Growing Up Gay in a Dysfunctional Family

Additional Titles by Rik Isensee

Love Between Men
We're Not Alone

Growing Up Gay in a Dysfunctional Family

▼

A Guide for Gay Men
Reclaiming Their Lives

Rik Isensee

PRENTICE
HALL
PARKSIDE

A PRENTICE HALL / PARKSIDE RECOVERY BOOK

New York   London   Toronto   Sydney   Tokyo   Singapore

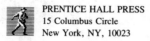 PRENTICE HALL PRESS
15 Columbus Circle
New York, NY, 10023

PRENTICE HALL PRESS and colophon are registered
trademarks of Simon & Schuster Inc.

Library of Congress Cataloging-in-Publication Data

Isensee, Rik.
    Growing up gay in a dysfunctional family : a guide for gay men
reclaiming their lives / Rik Isensee.
        p.   cm.
    ''A Prentice Hall/Parkside recovery book.''
    Includes bibliographical references (p. 216) and index.
    ISBN 0-13-346958-1
    1. Gay men—United States—Psychology.   2. Adult children of
dysfunctional families—United States.   I. Title.
HQ76.2.U5I838   1991
305.38'9664—dc20   91-13316
                                                             CIP

Designed by Richard Oriolo

Manufactured in the United States of America

10 9 8 7 6 5 4 3 2 1

First Edition

Parkside Medical Services Corporation is a full-service provider of treatment for
alcoholism, other drug addiction, eating disorders, and psychiatric illness.

Parkside Medical Services Corporation
205 West Touhy Avenue
Park Ride, IL 60068
1-800-PARKSIDE

The information in this book is not intended to replace the services
of a qualified professional. If you know or suspect that you have a
particular problem described in this book, you should consult a
professional.

Acknowledgments

▼

I am grateful to the following friends and colleagues who spent many hours reading this material and meeting with me to discuss their reactions. I gained so much from their suggestions, challenges, and encouragement, which stimulated and sustained me through numerous drafts: Wally Chapman; Albert Cota; Michael D'Arata, R.N.; Paul Fresina; Diane Gray, Ph.D.; David Hedden; John A. Martin, Ph.D.; Althea St. Amand; Tom Signore; and Larry Tyndall, Ph.D.

I had a number of clients in common with Dan Joy, L.C.S.W., a therapist in private practice. In our consultations, he provided me with keen insights and supported my work with gay male abuse survivors. He read the manuscript and contributed significantly to my perspective on male sexual abuse.

Although the focus of this book is on gay men, I owe a great deal to my women colleagues at the Center for Special Problems, an outpatient mental health clinic in San Francisco. When I came to the clinic, they had been offering therapy groups to female survivors of childhood abuse for several years. They welcomed me onto their team and helped me start a similar program for men. I developed the group described in chapter 11 under the guidance of my supervisor, Barbara Cook, R.N., L.C.S.W., who provided me with her expertise and generous support whenever I needed it. Mary-Perry Miller, Ph.D., and Susan Wachob, L.C.S.W., co-led some of the groups with me. I admire their clinical skill and sensitivity to issues confronting gay men in recovery. All three offered helpful suggestions for changes in the manuscript. Graduate students who co-led groups with me and brought their own expertise to our work together included Carol Gerstein, M.S.W.; Jeff Gold, Ph.D. candidate; Robert Meyers, M.S.; and Alexander Shaia, Ph.D. candidate.

I also ran a support group for gay, lesbian, and bisexual youth, some of whom had been abused or rejected by their families. Ruth

Acknowledgments

Hughes, B.S. candidate, director of the program for sexual minority youth, supported the group with her organizational skill and her network of community referrals. She and student coleaders Holly Gold, M.S.W.; Melissa Grossman, M.A.; and Deborah Yarock, M.A., helped me appreciate the impact of sex roles, ethnic differences, and family abuse on self-acceptance in gay and lesbian youth.

The following colleagues provided feedback in response to an early presentation on male sexual abuse. Through numerous discussions about similarities and differences between male and female abuse, they enriched my understanding of the influence of male socialization on gay male survivors: Alicia Carranza, L.C.S.W.; Lester Hazell, Ph.D.; Diane Kile, R.N., M.S.; Violet Ng, L.C.S.W.; Deborah Rochelle-Williams, L.C.S.W.; and Mary Tam Ma, L.C.S.W., team leader.

Thanks to Rinna Flohr, L.C.S.W., the director of the Center for Special Problems, who supported the development of services for male survivors and who kindly granted my leave of absence to complete this book; to my agent, Mitch Douglas at International Creative Management, for his support in developing this idea into a book proposal; and to my editor, Toni Sciarra, for her help in focusing what I was trying to say.

Finally, I am grateful to the dozens of gay men I have counseled over the last several years, who had the courage to confront and work through the effects of early abuse. They are the real experts on dysfunctional and homophobic families, and they have taught me a great deal about the process of healing through their willingness to share their experiences. Their determination, resilience, and perseverance demonstrate the potential for recovery that is possible when gay men reach out to one another for support. Witnessing their mutual encouragement and generosity inspired me to take on this project, and it is to their healing that I dedicate this book.

Contents
▼

Contents

Contents

Contents

Before You Begin
This Book

▼

As gay men, we have made great strides in our efforts to overcome homophobia in our society: We have challenged restrictive laws, formed coalitions with other progressive groups, and created an alternative culture to celebrate our diversity. We have also countered the assumption that the difficulties confronted by some gay men are a result of our sexual orientation. Low self-esteem, self-destructive behavior, and trouble with intimacy stem for the most part from the intense oppression we experience while growing up in dysfunctional families within a homophobic society. These problems are not *caused* by same-sex attractions.

The idea for this book was generated by my work with various groups of gay men: male couples, gay and bisexual youth, HIV-infected men, and men who were severely abused as children. Although these men are dealing with a wide range of issues, I noticed an underlying similarity between the post-traumatic effects reported by survivors of abusive families and some of the symptoms described by other gay men I have counseled.

The concept *post-traumatic stress* was developed to explain the symptoms that many soldiers experience after returning from combat, such as flashbacks, nightmares, and depression. Psychotherapists and other health providers have also recognized these symptoms in adult children of dysfunctional families. Emotional, physical, and sexual abuse can result in severe, long-lasting effects. Some of these symptoms include mistrust, withdrawal, anxiety, shame, and self-blame.

Growing up gay in a homophobic culture is comparable to growing up in a dysfunctional family: The shame and self-blame experienced by many gay youths are similar to the symptoms of abused children. As a result of this external threat, they may internalize a negative self-image that interferes with their ability to find meaningful work and form intimate relationships as gay adults.

I began to see that internalized homophobia is essentially a form of post-traumatic stress. Like former soldiers and abuse survivors, gay men often need to be hypervigilant, constantly on guard against potential assault. Homophobia and abusive families both contribute to anxiety, depression, and isolation. The resulting shame and low self-esteem that some gay men carry into adulthood can lead to self-destructive behavior.

Gay men in recovery from various addictions often get in touch with memories of early abuse. They realize that they have been using alcohol, drugs, food, or sex to escape from the memories and feelings that began to emerge from previous traumatic experiences. Although they may accept themselves as gay, they still feel affected by that early abuse and the resultant internalized homophobia. Some fear failure or sabotage their success, and they seek help because they are not living up to their true potential.

Working through past abuse is an important resource for countering internalized homophobia and healing ourselves. In my therapy groups for men abused as children, we deal with the post-traumatic effects of physical, sexual, and homophobic abuse. The men in these groups provide one another with the recognition and understanding that they seldom receive from their families. They discover that they have a lot in common with other gay men who have had similar experiences, and this helps them understand current symptoms as normal reactions to early trauma, instead of assuming that something is inherently wrong with them. They may still see ways in which they would like to change, but they feel released from much of the self-blame that contributed to their low self-esteem and self-defeating behavior. Understanding this process has generated hope and motivation among the men in my groups, so I decided to put these ideas together in a form that gay men could use on their own to supplement their recovery programs.

The book is divided into two parts. Part I, ''Homophobia and Trauma,'' looks at what it's like to grow up gay in a homophobic culture and compares these effects to the post-traumatic symptoms that often occur in response to dysfunctional families. It also links homophobia with the cycle of shame to explain its role in maintaining four types of self-destructive behavior: addictions, compulsions, self-deprivation, and codependence. Recovery from substance abuse and compulsive behavior will help you address your underlying feelings and reactions to previous trauma.

Part II, ''Reclaiming Your Life,'' describes various aspects of healing: insight about internalized oppression, working through feelings, countering negative messages, self-nurturing, and reaching out for support. Insight can help you understand how you may have absorbed homophobic and other negative messages from your family and from the surrounding culture. Self-nurturing can help you replace negative self-talk with soothing encouragement. Emotional support can help you work through the feelings that arise when you make changes in your behavior.

You may find ways in which your own experience differs from the examples in this book. These thoughts are not intended to be all-inclusive, but rather to indicate a range of possible influences. The end of each chapter provides suggestions for relating this material to your own experience. You might want to keep a journal of the memories and feelings that are stimulated by these ideas. Writing down your reactions will give you an overview of how you coped with the dynamics in your family, how you may have developed self-defeating patterns, and how you can break the cycle of shame to heal from previous abuse. It also helps to talk about your reactions with people who understand what you are going through: your support group, your therapist, or other friends in recovery.

This book clarifies the link between homophobia and post-traumatic symptoms and provides a systematic guide for recovery from dysfunctional and homophobic families. It will help you understand the process you are going through as you heal from early trauma, internalized homophobia, and addictions. It also can help you heal from homophobic assaults as an adult. You'll learn how to handle conflicts and problems without blaming yourself or trying to escape your feelings through drugs or self-defeating behavior. As you heal from previous trauma, you will gain the freedom to create your own life.

A Note of Caution

This book is intended to complement psychotherapy, group therapy, and self-help programs for gay men who are working on memories and feelings related to early abuse, homophobia, and recovery from addictions or compulsive behavior. Many of the ideas contained in this book are derived from my work with gay men who were abused as children. If you were abused, understanding the basis of your tumultuous feelings and reactions can help alleviate self-blame and shame and assist you in the process of healing.

However, if you are in early recovery from alcohol or substance abuse, you may want to concentrate on staying clean and sober for six months to a year before delving into underlying family problems. When you read about the effects of early abuse in part 1 of this book, you may get in touch with memories that are difficult to deal with in the initial phase of recovery. It takes time to learn how to handle the feelings that begin to emerge after you stop abusing alcohol or other drugs. Once you are well established in your recovery program, childhood memories often emerge spontaneously. You can explore these memories in psychotherapy or in a group that focuses on early childhood abuse.

Even if you have a lot of experience in recovery, it can still be overwhelming to read through this book all at once. Read a section or two at a time, and then take a break to write down your reactions. If you find yourself flooded by painful memories and feelings, it is vital that you get some support before you continue. Talk to someone who understands what you are going through and who can help you make sense of early memories: your therapist, support group, or an understanding friend.

Part I

Homophobia
and
Trauma

1

Growing Up Gay in a Homophobic Culture

Imagine what it would be like to grow up in a society in which same-sex attractions were considered perfectly normal—if you held hands with another little boy, your relatives might tease you about having a boyfriend, but they'd think you were cute. In junior high, you could chatter on the phone with your friends to get up enough courage to ask the new boy in class to the school dance. In high school, you could greet your boyfriend backstage with flowers for his performance in the school play, give him a kiss during baseball practice, go to the prom, or neck in the woods—all without fear of being harassed, shamed, assaulted, or shunned. When you set out on your own, you might eventually meet a man and fall in love. You could bring him home to meet your parents so they could celebrate your relationship and welcome him into your family.

Although a few young gays in urban areas are beginning to experience some of these freedoms, we obviously have a long way to go before such a care-free existence becomes a reality for most gay people. The level of homophobia that permeates our culture makes it difficult for gay youth to develop a confident self-image. It can also restrain our enthusiasm even when we accept ourselves and share our love with another man. In this chapter, we will look at what it's like to grow up gay within a homophobic culture and explore the impact of homophobia on assuming a gay identity.

Homophobia and Heterosexism

Homophobia is the expression of prejudice against homosexuality in general, and toward gay people in particular.[1] The term *heterosexism* has also been used to refer to the heterosexual bias that institutionalizes heterosexual norms and discriminates against gay people. Homophobic and heterosexist attitudes may be expressed through individual prejudice, institutional discrimination, and internalized homophobia.

Individual Prejudice

Why should the fact that we are open to loving relationships with other men be such a threat to heterosexuals? Individual prejudice can be influenced by the following factors:[2]

- Ignorance and lack of experience with gay people
- Conflicts with other beliefs and values
- Conformity to social norms
- Denial and projection of internal conflicts

Ignorance and lack of experience with gay people. Some people are ignorant about what gay people are really like. They think they've never met a gay person, or the only people they identify as gay are those who fit certain stereotypes. People who are simply uninformed are more likely to alter their beliefs about gays when they actually have a chance to meet and talk with someone who is openly gay, or when they find out that someone they already know and respect is gay. However, simply knowing a gay person may not be sufficient to change personal attitudes. The *quality* of contact has a major influence on changing or reinforcing prejudice. We will explore this idea further in chapter 12.

Conflicts with other beliefs and values. People who have religious beliefs or other values that require a specific attitude toward homosexuality may not be easily influenced by new information or contact with gays. A Catholic mother, for example, may not have thought much about homosexuality, but accepts the church's condemnation of homosexual relationships. However, finding out her son is gay creates an emotional conflict: She loves her son and knows that he is a wonderful person, yet her church teaches that homosexual contact is a sin. She may ease her pain by compartmentalizing her thoughts about her son: Rather than changing her beliefs, she may think of her son as asexual—or more likely, she doesn't think about her son's sexuality at all.

Other values may also mitigate her negative attitude toward her son's sexual orientation: She may believe in his right to privacy or that it's not up to her to judge others. She may also believe that it is important for her to support her own son, even if she doesn't approve of his lifestyle. Meeting other religious parents who have reconciled their beliefs with homosexuality may also help her accept her son's sexual orientation.

Conformity to social norms. Some people are influenced by what's considered acceptable within their circle of friends. They may make fun of gays because everyone around them has a similar attitude. Having friends who talk about the issues that gay people face, who disapprove of homophobic comments or jokes, and who include gays at social events may cause a shift in their attitude toward homosexuality. If their prejudices or misconceptions are not firmly rooted, they may alter their opinions to conform to those of their social network. Peer pressure in this regard can be very influential, even if the change is somewhat superficial.

Denial and projection of internal conflicts. People whose prejudice serves a psychological function in their personality are less likely to change their views on homosexuality. This group includes men who feel conflicted about their own homosexual desires, those who feel threatened by any challenge to traditional masculine roles, and those who are confused and insecure about sexual feelings in general.[3] People tend not to recognize things they dislike about themselves. Instead, they project these negative qualities onto others. Gays are often seen as promiscuous; we are depicted as child molesters; we are blamed for the spread of AIDS; and we are held responsible for the breakdown of marriage, sexual morals, and the family.

Prejudice against gays, women, and ethnic minorities probably represents a disowned, unconscious side of men who feel insecure about their sexuality, their masculinity, and their place in the world. Homophobic men may feel threatened by our transgression of rigid social roles because it challenges their shaky self-concept of what it means to be a man, or it awakens their forbidden desires. They see the threat coming from the outside, rather than recognizing their own impulses and ambivalence.

Institutionalized Discrimination

Homophobia is not just a problem of individual prejudice; it is reflected in many of our institutions: churches, schools, sports, media, courts, and the military. The institutionalization of homophobia reinforces interpersonal prejudice and limits the civil rights of gay people. When prejudice is supported by the major institutions of a society, it becomes a group norm. Homophobic jokes, harassment, and even violence may elicit tacit approval from others.[4] Listed below are some of the ways in which homophobia has been legitimized by various institutions in the United States.

In many states, sex between men is still illegal. Some states prohibit oral or anal intercourse, whether practiced by heterosexual couples or gays, and some states specifically outlaw homosexual contact. This form of state-sponsored harassment has been upheld by the U.S. Supreme Court.[5] Since it is difficult to claim protection for an illegal activity, this ruling has undermined efforts to establish civil rights for gay people in states where same-sex contact is prohibited.

Gay relationships are not recognized by the state. Even in the states where sex between men is legal, we are not allowed to marry. Our parenting rights are often challenged and we have no guarantee of spousal benefits such as tax breaks, inheritance, or the right to make medical decisions when one's partner is incapacitated.[6]

Gay people are subject to legal discrimination. Our rights to employment, housing, and privacy have been established in very few states or local jurisdictions. In some of the cities that have passed antidiscriminatory legislation, the laws have been repealed.

Gays are seen as being disruptive to military service. Gays are barred from enlisting, and they may be expelled from military service if their sexual orientation is discovered. Before World War II, African Americans were excluded from serving with whites, under the assumption that no white man would take orders from someone he considered inferior. Similar arguments are made today that gays would threaten discipline and morale.[7] It is assumed that the male bonding that takes place in combat would be jeopardized if its potential for erotic contact were condoned. The military also uses the rationale that gays are subject to blackmail, even though men who are openly gay have nothing to hide.

Fear of AIDS has become a vehicle for discriminatory and sex-negative legislation.[8] Laws protecting persons with AIDS from discrimination in jobs and housing have been repealed in a number of communities; children, families, and gay men with AIDS have been attacked; gay bath houses and other meeting places have been closed down.

Homophobic attacks on the arts and media limit freedom of expression. Gay people in the media are often depicted as sensational stereotypes. When the media offer a rare glimpse of authentic gay lifestyles, they are bombarded with homophobic protests and threats to cut advertising support. Public slurs and ridicule are commonly tolerated, whereas positive depiction is decried as promotion and recruitment.[9]

Many religious denominations condemn homosexual relations. The Catholic church has condemned homosexuality by claiming that same-sex relationships are an "objective disorder."[10] They will not approve of condom use or safe-sex education practices other than abstinence. The Traditional Values Coalition and other religious groups regularly oppose antidiscriminatory legislation.[11] Although homosexuality is no longer considered a mental disorder by mental health professionals, some religious groups try to recruit and convert conflicted young gays with "cures" for homosexuality.[12]

Violent attacks against gays are excused by "homosexual panic." Though hate-motivated crimes have been identified as one of the leading causes of violence against gays, many gay men are reluctant to report violent attacks because they fear being harassed by the police or exposed through a court trial. Victims of violence are often accused of bringing the violence on themselves simply by being gay.[13]

Schools discriminate against homosexuality. There is little mention of homosexuality in sex education classes. References to gay historical figures often omit the fact that they were gay and that their sexual orientation had a major influence on their work. Same-sex couples are often prohibited from attending school dances. Slurs, sexual harassment, and physical assaults against gays (or students perceived to be gay) are frequently tolerated.

All of these types of institutionalized discrimination reinforce and legitimize prejudice in homophobic individuals. How can individuals change when the surrounding culture reinforces their prejudice? This quandary is one of the primary difficulties we face in trying to combat homophobia in our society.[14]

How Homophobia Becomes Internalized

Since gay men grow up in the same culture as heterosexuals, we are just as susceptible to homophobic beliefs as everyone else. Most of the time, when people feel threatened, they protect their self-esteem by valuing themselves and deflecting the negative input that attacks their self-esteem.[15] So how do we end up internalizing the homophobia of the surrounding culture? Homophobic oppression requires four components in order to become internalized:

- Prejudice
- Misinformation
- Isolation
- Heterosexual bias

The first three qualities contribute to the internalization of a negative self-image in any group that is discriminated against.[16] In addition, gay men also have to deal with the invisibility caused by the pervasive heterosexual bias that permeates our culture. By recognizing how these components operate together in society and in our lives, we can take active steps to create a healthier self-image as adults. Let's examine each one in greater detail.

Prejudice. Internalized homophobia stems directly from the external homophobia we face every day. Systematic oppression makes it extremely difficult to feel good about our sexuality while growing up. We learn very early that our true feelings are dangerous to expose to anyone. Homophobia thus creates an environment of secrecy and shame that interferes with normal adolescent development and inhibits the formation of a positive gay identity. If we were accepted and appreciated, we'd no doubt have many of the same struggles with intimacy that heterosexuals experience in modern society, but *we'd be less likely to assume that our problems arose simply because we love another man.*

Misinformation. We grow up with the same misconceptions about homosexuality that straight people do. Our culture is permeated with the assumption that homosexuality is sinful or sick. The falsehoods, perpetuated by the media, churches, and our schools, are so pervasive that young people rarely question them. It's dangerous to let anyone know that they think homosexuality is all right, lest they be identified as gay themselves. Because of our own lack of knowledge it is easy to assume that *something is wrong with us* when we first become aware of same-sex attractions.

Isolation. Members of ethnic groups that are discriminated against often look to their families and communities for solace, identity, and support. For young gays, however, it's difficult to identify other gay people. We are often cut off from any source of nurturing, recognition, or acceptance. Ethnic gays have the added burden of trying to balance gay and ethnic identities. They face potential disapproval or rejection by their own ethnic group and frequently confront racist attitudes in the gay community.

Our invisibility is both a blessing and a hindrance: If we can pass as heterosexual, we may be able to escape much of the harassment that we would experience if others knew that we were gay. Yet our invisibility, while it keeps us safe, can also keep us from finding other men who have similar feelings. We need positive interactions with peers like ourselves in order to counter the negative messages we have absorbed. The conflict between our emerging sexuality and a healthy self-concept can lead to denial or self-hatred. Denial of our feelings can make us avoid other gays because they might elicit our attraction. We may also be hesitant to reach out for support from gay groups for fear of being ostracized by our straight friends.

Heterosexual bias. In addition to isolation, gays face another obstacle: silence. Even though homosexuality has gotten a lot more press in recent years (largely because of AIDS), it is rarely discussed or acknowledged with any depth of understanding. Discussions about family policies ignore gay and lesbian families, the special needs of older or disabled gays are rarely addressed, and the effects of discrimination on minority gays are given little attention. Studies of adolescent suicide neglect the homophobic source of many teenagers' isolation and despair.[17]

Even when we are not being *directly* harassed or discriminated against, society's heterosexist message to gays is that we don't exist or that we are freaks—subhuman and unmentionable.[18] Unless we have some positive experiences that can counter these beliefs and assumptions, we may feel ashamed by our very existence.

Are Gay Men Really Different?

To understand the effects of growing up gay in a homophobic culture, it's helpful to look at some of our assumptions about how gay or bisexual men differ from heterosexuals. Evelyn Hooker's research in the 1950s compared the results of psychological tests on groups of gay and heterosexual men. There was no substantial difference between the two groups in terms of how well they functioned, and it was not possible to tell who was gay and who was straight on the basis of their test scores.[19]

This finding was a revelation to many psychiatrists who had based their assumption of homosexual pathology on their work with gay men in treatment, many of whom felt bad about being gay. It was the first evaluation of gay men who accepted their orientation and felt fine about themselves. Hooker's work inspired other researchers to replicate her studies, and in 1973 homosexuality was removed from the American Psychiatric Association's list of mental disorders.

Research also has discounted the theory that gays have dominant mothers and distant fathers. *There is no strong predictor in early family life for the development of sexual orientation, gay or straight.* In Bell and Weinberg's study of sexual preference, the only difference they found was that many boys who became gay men exhibited "gender nonconformity."[20] Their findings also challenged the assumption of a causal relationship between "effeminacy" and a distant father: "Whether a failure to identify with one's father encourages effeminacy, or whether boys who for whatever reason happen to be effeminate find it difficult to identify with their fathers" remains ambiguous.[21]

Many gay men report that their fathers abandoned them emotionally when they didn't conform to male role expectations. In a psychoanalytic analysis of gay male development, Richard Isay suggests that our fathers distance themselves from us because they sense our attraction to them.[22] Another possibility might be that the father of a son who seems sensitive or different may not be sure how to relate to him, so he withdraws. The boy doesn't know why he is being rejected, so he assumes that there must be something wrong with him.

As the boy grows older and becomes aware of same-sex attractions, he tends to hide his feelings. Because it's not safe to let anyone know how he feels, he suffers isolation and alienation. This may be reinforced by negative interactions with his father and other boys, who may imply that he isn't really a man if he's not interested in girls, or if he cannot excel in sports. Of course, not all gay boys dislike sports, and not all straight boys conform to masculine roles. But we learn very early that certain behaviors are expected if we want to be accepted.

Many homophobic put-downs—sissy, femme, wimp, fairy, effeminate—derive from men's fear of being associated with women. Even being sensitive and artistic is suspect, because *real* men are not expected to be overly sensitive. Being like a woman is the ultimate insult to men who are insecure about their own masculinity. Gay men seem to be graced with the capacity for a wide range of sex-role behaviors that exhibit themselves in many boys long before they have any idea that they are transcending traditional male roles, and before they even realize that they are attracted to men.[23]

The word *effeminacy* perpetuates stereotypical male and female roles. What is masculine or feminine behavior apart from how we've been socialized? Rigid roles inhibit every person's capacity for a wide range of behaviors that needn't be limited by gender.

Homophobia inhibits relationships and interactions between *all* men, not just between straight and gay men.[24] Men often are hesitant to touch one another except through rough play and tend not to reveal feelings of vulnerability to their friends. Other cultures have a wider range of acceptable masculine behavior: Men can hug, kiss, and hold hands without anyone questioning their masculinity.

While women are socialized to place the needs of others ahead of their own interests, men are socialized to take any step that will give them a competitive advantage. Many gay men reject these rigid roles, but it takes a lot of conscious effort to counter this conditioning in order to reach out in loving relationships with other men.

Gay men are frequently asked why we feel the need to make a point of our homosexuality. Our desire for male recognition and affection is not too different from that of straight men, although heterosexual men often repress these feelings. The main difference is that gays are interested in expanding their affection into sexual and loving relationships with other men. Many of us would have been perfectly happy to fall in love with our best friends without ever feeling the need to identify ourselves as being different. We have been forced, however, to defend ourselves in response to the intolerance that we encounter. Lacking support from our families or peers, it helps to identify with other gay men so we can make sense of our experience and realize that we are not alone. Reclaiming our hidden history enables us to affirm our existence and take pride in our creative adaptations to an aversive environment.

Establishing a Gay Identity

Given the homophobic attitudes of the surrounding culture, how does a gay youth establish a positive identity as a gay adult? Adolescence is a transition from a child's total dependence on the family to an adult status of financial and psychological independence. It can be an exciting time of trying out new roles, values, and sexual experiments. As a young man establishes affectionate peer relationships, he gradually forms an identity separate from his parents. He prepares himself for the life-long tasks of getting along with others, finding meaningful work, and establishing intimate relationships. If he negotiates these tasks successfully, he also forms a healthy relationship with himself, discovering a sense of meaning and purpose in his life.

Most young people undergo this transition with a great deal of anxiety and self-consciousness, but they manage somehow to muddle through. For gay youths, adolescence can be an especially treacherous time. Peer support—the young person's major ally during this transition to adulthood—is only minimally available to gay youths. An openly gay young man may arouse anxiety and anger in other males by touching on their own fears of same-sex attraction or desires for affection.

Normal adolescent development includes the following tasks in preparation for adulthood:

1. Separate from parents and form peer relationships
2. Develop friendships
3. Assume a sexual orientation
4. Begin sexual exploration and intimate relationships
5. Establish one's own identity

Everyone "grows up gay" differently. As you read about each transitional task, try to remember how *you* negotiated these developmental milestones.

1. Separate from parents and form peer relationships. The transition from dependency to autonomy in our culture is more rigidly defined for boys than for girls, who are often able to admit their insecurities and confide in their friends (and sometimes in their mothers) throughout adolescence. Girls are able to touch, brush one another's hair, say they like one another, and sleep in the same bed without anyone being suspicious of their sexual orientation. Boys, however, learn that they are supposed to inhibit any expression of tenderness and sensitivity toward other males, especially after puberty. Affection tends to be interpreted as weakness and often is associated with homosexuality, regardless of any underlying sexual attraction. Adolescent boys may desire recognition and approval from other males, but they can no longer ask for nurturing directly. They rarely admit self-doubt to other boys for fear that they be seen as needy or dependent.

Coming out as gay may seem like a perfect form of adolescent rebellion, but most gay youths lack a peer group that would reinforce and support a gay identity. Unless he is lucky enough to have an understanding adult in his life or he's able to make friends with other gays, the gay youth deals with most of his confusion and self-doubt by himself.

2. Develop friendships. Even when other young gays or support groups are available, a gay youth may feel too threatened to associate with them. The conflict between his desire for acceptance by other boys and his dimly realized homosexual orientation may inhibit the development of close friendships, because he doesn't feel safe enough to disclose his true feelings. To cover his anxiety over being discovered he may pretend to be heterosexual.

3. Assume a sexual orientation. Discovering one's sexual orientation is a significant task for everyone, whether he or she is gay, straight, or bisexual. Until recently, however, assuming a *heterosexual* identity and role has been seen as the primary task, with homosexual or bisexual interests either considered deviant or ignored altogether.[25]

A gay youth risks rejection and assault if he is open about his orientation, yet if he keeps quiet, he remains completely isolated. He tends to blame himself either way: If he's harassed, he gets angry with himself for not being able to pass as straight; yet if he doesn't let anyone get to know him, he may feel lonely and blame himself for not fitting in. It is difficult for him to recognize that whatever problems he has as a result of his isolation and fear of exposure are not caused by his sexual orientation but by the threat of homophobic discrimination.

4. Begin sexual exploration and intimate relationships. A gay youth does not have the freedom to explore his sexuality within an accepting and nurturing environment. He may feel excluded from the bragging of other boys about their sexual exploits and either keep quiet or feel compelled to lie. Although the other boys are probably lying too, their lies and exaggerations are about heterosexual fantasies that the gay youth doesn't share.

Infatuation is a form of testing one's own identity by yearning for a loved one and fantasizing that the loved one will respond favorably. A young person learns how to appreciate himself as a sexual being by imagining himself through another's eyes. Yet the gay youth's infatuations often remain secret, tinged with his fear of rejection. Instead of imagining a flattering response, he may anticipate loathing from the boys he admires.

If he misses out on the normal adolescent fumbling with peers, he may find more secretive outlets through masturbation with erotica or through casual sex with older males, which may leave him vulnerable to sexual abuse and to AIDS and other sexually transmitted diseases. He may also feel a great deal of shame as a result of his secret life. Furtive sexual contacts may inhibit his ability to initiate or accept a caring emotional relationship. Feeling excluded from close friendships and missing out on emotionally involved sexuality may hamper the development of his capacity for intimacy.

5. Establish one's own identity. Identity formation is an ongoing task, even after we reach adulthood. Young people frequently try on many beliefs about sex, ethics, religion, and politics. They experiment with different vocational interests and lifestyles to discover who they are and what they really value.

For gay young men, this exploration may be inhibited by the fear of rejection. Lacking support from peers or role models they can identify with, they may try dating girls. Some boys become slovenly or overweight, perhaps as an unconscious strategy to avoid being expected to compete for girls or in athletics. Other boys may withdraw from peer activities altogether. Some gay youths find acceptance in alienated groups that use drugs or drop out of school. Any of these strategies, though they certainly make sense for short-term survival in a hostile environment, may result in delayed development of a strong identity.

Phases in Self-Acceptance

Even without much peer support, many gay men do come to terms with their sexual orientation by their early twenties. In recent years, some urban youths have more freely accepted different lifestyles, allowing a few young gays to explore their sexuality in a more nurturing environment.

In this section, we'll look at how a youth develops a positive gay identity. These phases are not intended to predict anyone's path of self-acceptance, but you can get an idea of the variety of reactions encountered by many gay youths as they come to terms with their sexual orientation.[26] The path to gay identity may include the following phases:

1. Awareness of gender nonconformity
2. Conflict over self-image
3. Confusion and shame
4. Denial and projection
5. Rationalizing
6. Trying to change
7. Mourning the loss of a heterosexual self-image
8. Acceptance
9. Coming out
10. Forming gay relationships

Let's look at how each of these phases affects (and is affected by) the developmental tasks listed previously.

1. Awareness of gender nonconformity. Even before a young boy consciously realizes that he has same-sex attractions, he may encounter feedback from the environment that he is somehow different and that this difference puts him in grave jeopardy. Even before he can understand the words *gender role nonconformity,* the message becomes quite clear that he risks rejection, taunts, and assault for any deviation from the behavior of other boys.

It should be pointed out that not all boys who don't conform to masculine stereotypes turn out to be gay, and many gay men never felt "different" when they were children. Some don't realize until adolescence that they are attracted to other males, yet with this realization comes the harsh discovery that same-sex attractions are a serious violation of gender roles.

2. Conflict over self-image. A gay youth hears words like fag, queer, or homo before he knows what they mean. He gradually becomes aware that these derogatory terms refer to his feelings of attraction for other males. This realization creates conflict—he has sexual and loving feelings toward his friends, but he has learned to associate these feelings with illness, sin, and disgust.

3. Confusion and shame. Not wanting to be perceived as being sick, bad, or disgusting, a gay youth may become very confused because he still has these strange attractions despite his desire to be rid of them. Since he continues to be attracted to other males, he may accept the conclusion that he *is* sick and disgusting. Fearing discovery, he may hide his feelings. Alternatively, some boys assume that if they are gay they have to dress or talk in a certain way or be sexually available to other boys.

4. Denial and projection. If a gay youth denies his "disgusting" feelings, he may still be preoccupied with them. He might try to hide his sexual confusion with jokes about queers or insult his friends when they exhibit any tenderness or affection that elicits his own feelings of attraction. Accusing another boy of being a fag is one way to protect himself from any suspicion that he might be gay. Some gay youths may even participate in gay-bashing in order to prove that they are really heterosexual.

5. Rationalizing. Following a same-sex experience, a gay youth might assume that homosexuality is only a phase—he was just horny, and there wasn't a girl available. If he has a crush on a best friend, he may think that it is only this particular friend that he really likes and that it doesn't necessarily mean that he's gay—maybe he's bisexual. Some men really are bisexual; however, many young people find it easier to identify themselves as bisexual before they fully accept their same-sex attractions.

6. Trying to change. After a while, a gay youth may recognize that he is homosexual, but he wants to change. He might pray, forswear masturbation, avoid magazines that arouse him, and turn off TV shows that refer to homosexuality. He tries going out with girls, or even gets married. He might seek counseling from a pastor, a family friend, or a psychotherapist. If he finds someone who can guide him through his feelings, he may come to terms with his sexual orientation. If people dismiss his feelings by reassuring him that he's not really gay, if he is rejected in horror, or if persons in authority try to change him—or attempt to seduce him—he becomes even more confused.

7. Mourning the loss of a heterosexual self-image. When a gay youth's efforts to change don't work, he can no longer deny that he's attracted to men, but he still may feel bad about it. This is a dangerous stage: A young man at this juncture is close to acceptance but very vulnerable to suicide. He feels hopeless about changing, yet he cannot conceive that he could ever feel good about himself as a gay person.

8. Acceptance. Acceptance often is facilitated by meeting other gay men, which can dispel a lot of negative images and stereotypes. The gay youth learns that all kinds of men are gay and that he doesn't have to conform to a certain image. A positive sexual experience with a male partner that includes some emotional caring may affirm his attraction to men.

9. Coming out. Acknowledging his sexual orientation to himself is the first step in coming out. A man may gradually disclose his orientation to a larger circle of friends, both gay and straight. As he feels more comfortable with his identity, he may choose to tell his family. Coming out is a lifelong process. In every new situation that we encounter, we need to choose whether to disclose our sexual orientation.

10. Forming gay relationships. Acceptance and coming out often lead to the reemergence of earlier adolescent identity issues, which may explain the ''second adolescent'' sexual experimentation of many gay men. A young man who is just coming out may go through the developmental milestones that he missed as an adolescent, this time within a more accepting environment: He consolidates his separation from his family, develops intimate friendships with peers, and becomes more comfortable with his sexual orientation. He gradually learns how to make contact with other men, how to date, how to initiate sex, how to let someone know when he's interested and when he's not. He learns how to listen, how to state what he wants, and how to negotiate his needs. As he feels more confident in his ability to reach out to others, he establishes a positive sense of himself as a young man who happens to be gay.

Relating These Ideas to Your Own Experience

In this section, you can consider how your own experience resembles or differs from the descriptions in this chapter. You may want to keep a journal of the memories and feelings that are stimulated by these ideas.

- What was it like for you to grow up gay in your own neighborhood, school, and family?
- How did homophobic or heterosexist attitudes affect you when you were a boy? How do they influence your feelings and attitudes now?
- In what ways have you been aware of or subjected to prejudice, misinformation, isolation, or heterosexual bias?
- When did you first realize that you were attracted to other males?
- Was there anyone you could talk to about your feelings or did you keep them secret?
- Who was the first person you ever told about being gay, and how did he or she respond?
- Trace your own journey toward acceptance. How did it differ from the stages outlined above? What was it like for you to realize that you felt attracted to some of your male friends?
- Are you "out" to your family? How are they dealing with it? If you haven't told them, how do you feel about not telling them?
- How do you feel about your sexual orientation now? How have your feelings changed over time?

2

▼

Dysfunctional and
Abusive Families

Children are dependent on their parents for meeting such obvious needs as food, clothing, and shelter, but they also need their *feelings* and *experience* to be understood and appreciated. This acceptance helps a child feel comforted and confident as he discovers his own talents and capabilities. He has a sense that he is loved for who he is and not simply for what he can provide for his parents.

Much of the recent literature on dysfunctional families describes the deleterious effects of abuse on child development.[1] The normal growth of a child is distorted in order to conform to the needs of a dysfunctional family. In this chapter, we will explore how a well-functioning family encourages the development of a positive self-image. We will contrast healthy development with the problems encountered by a gay boy growing up in a dysfunctional, abusive, or homophobic family.

Origins of a Positive
Self-Image

We all need a positive image of ourselves in order to develop meaningful work and intimate relationships. A healthy self-concept develops naturally in a nurturing family where the child is respected for his thoughts and feelings. A child is born with four basic needs:

- Dependable nurturing
- Unconditional love
- Empathy
- Acceptance and recognition

If all four of these needs are met, the child has a greater chance of developing a positive self-image.

Dependable nurturing. A child depends on his parents to take care of him by providing food, clothing, and shelter. Besides needing to be cared for and kept safe, he also needs to be touched, hugged, and held with warm, nonsexual affection. If he feels frightened or overwhelmed, he needs comfort and reassurance.

Unconditional love. Being loved unconditionally means that a child is loved even when his parents are upset by his behavior. If his parents can love him simply because he is their child, he develops a sense of well-being and self-worth. He doesn't have to accomplish anything or prove himself to feel worthy. Although his parents need to set reasonable limits on his behavior, he can play and eat, get cranky and sleep, make a mess or throw a tantrum and still know that he is loved.

Empathy. Empathy is the ability to communicate an understanding of another person's feelings. Empathic parents have access to their own memories and feelings from childhood, so they can imagine what it must be like for a child to be totally dependent. They don't feel threatened by his expression of unhappiness. Instead, they let him know that they understand how frustrating it can be to experience all the limitations that a child is faced with. A parent who can accept and acknowledge a child's various moods (such as sorrow, clinging, rage, and eventual needs for separation) allows him to experience his emotions within an environment of love and security.

Acceptance and recognition. Every child needs to have his own unique feelings, thoughts, and experiences accepted and valued. Parents who take delight in their child's natural growth foster self-confidence and inspire the development of his true capabilities. He feels free to explore his talents and dreams because his parents aren't threatened by his self-expression. They don't demand that he have certain thoughts, feelings, or beliefs in order to be acceptable, nor do they require that he continue his dependence on them.

A healthy family sets rules and limits that reflect the developmental abilities of the child. A child may feel frustrated when he doesn't get what he wants, but he's not punished for expressing his disappointment. Conflicts are negotiated to address everyone's needs. Family members talk about their experiences and share their dreams for the future. Children and adults feel comfortable with some time apart and also seek out one another's company. The child feels secure in the knowledge that he can depend on his parents to take care of him and love him.

Self-absorption is a natural stage in a child's development. As an infant, he assumes he is the center of the world. As he matures, he comes to understand that he can't always be the focus of his parents' attention, nor can he always depend on his parents for nurturing and guidance. He gradually increases his tolerance for frustration and learns how to nurture himself. When his needs for nurturing, love, empathy, and acceptance are met at an early age, he is less likely to become preoccupied with fulfilling these needs as an adult.

Parents aren't always able to respond to their child's disappointments with compassion, especially if they are preoccupied with their own concerns. Fortunately, they don't have to be perfect in order for their child to develop a healthy self-image.[2] Occasionally feeling overwhelmed by the demands of a child is natural for parents, but they can let their child know they still love him once they calm down. The basic sense that the child is cherished for his own sake is communicated through the parents' emotional accessibility over a period of years.

With this positive core, a child's self-esteem is not imperiled by feeling sad or disappointed. He learns how to maintain both positive and negative feelings about himself and others: When he is disappointed, he neither blames himself too harshly nor sees other people as being all good or all bad. Because his own feelings have been understood and accepted, he is able to empathize with others. He also can temper his impulses and needs by recognizing the impact of his actions. A gay boy who grows up in such a family may be able to express his emerging sexual orientation in an atmosphere of support and respect for his individuality.

In contrast to the love and acceptance of a well-functioning family, let's take a look at how growing up in a dysfunctional family leaves these basic needs unmet. We will also see how the particular ways in which gay boys are often abused can reinforce a negative self-image.

Dysfunctional Families Defined

The concept of the dysfunctional family grew out of recovery work by adult children of alcoholic families. It became apparent that an alcoholic family member doesn't drink in isolation. His or her partner and the children become enmeshed in a system that tends to reinforce alcoholic behavior. Alcoholism is not a prerequisite for a dysfunctional family, though it often contributes to battering, child abuse, and incest. The concept of the dysfunctional family has been broadened to include a range of abusive interactions, whether or not alcoholism or substance abuse is a contributing factor. These include emotional, physical, and sexual abuse, as well as the neglect of physical and emotional needs.

Aside from alcohol and substance abuse, other contributors to parental inadequacy include social problems, isolation, and ignorance about parenting skills. Parents often feel frustrated and overwhelmed by the task of child-rearing in a society that doesn't provide much support for child care. The disruption of previous social networks, such as extended families and cohesive communities, has left many families isolated from friends or relatives who could help out during emergencies. When parents face major problems such as unemployment, illness, or the breakup of a marriage, they may take out some of their frustration on their children. Parents who lack knowledge about normal child development also may be inconsistent in setting necessary limits or may make unrealistic demands, such as expecting a child to be toilet-trained too early.

Listed below are some common traits of dysfunctional families. An occasional parental failure doesn't necessarily mean that your family is dysfunctional, nor will every dysfunctional family display all of these traits. Some families are very rigid, for example, while others are chaotic. Some families suppress feelings, while others vent uncontrolled rage. What dysfunctional families have in common is a pervasive pattern of ignoring or discounting the child's feelings, often combined with abusive interactions. Whether chaotic, violent, rigid, or intrusive, *dysfunctional families consistently fail the child's need for dependable nurturing, unconditional love, empathy, and acceptance.* We'll discuss each trait in detail and describe how these characteristics are likely to affect a gay child growing up in a dysfunctional family.

- Intrusive
- Stereotypical gender roles
- Violation of trust
- Inconsistent
- Mixed messages
- Chaotic
- Rigid
- Isolated
- Secretive
- Lack of communication
- Suppression of feelings
- Uncontrolled rage
- Denial of addictive behavior

- Scapegoating
- Children take on adult responsibilities
- Children develop symptoms to protect their parents

Intrusive. Parents in dysfunctional families have a poor sense of physical and psychological boundaries. They may enter their children's rooms without knocking even after their children have reached adolescence. A gay youth in such a family has no place in which he has any privacy for exploring his emerging feelings. Parents or siblings may walk in on him while he is masturbating. They may read his mail or diary, eavesdrop on phone calls, or search his room for forbidden books and magazines.

Stereotypical gender roles. The parents in a dysfunctional family may subscribe to stereotypical masculine and feminine roles. The father may keep his feelings to himself, rarely disclosing any emotional vulnerability. The mother may try to make up for her husband's unavailability by becoming overinvolved with her children. Rigid roles may be enforced among the children: Boys are told not to cry and are forbidden to play with dolls; girls are expected to help their mothers and not show any interest in athletics. A gay boy who displays any nontypical interests may be ignored or ridiculed for not conforming to male pursuits.

Violation of trust. Parents may violate each other's trust through having affairs, doing drug deals, or squandering family income. They may lie to the children, betray confidences, and not follow through on commitments. A gay son learns that he must not disclose his true feelings, doubts, or confusion about his sexuality or he will be betrayed.

Inconsistent. Rules and expectations may be inconsistent and arbitrary, depending on the parents' moods and whims. "Because I said so" is enough reason to obey any dictum, regardless of what was said yesterday or what will be said tomorrow. Parents may disagree about rules, but instead of talking about their disagreement, they may undermine each other's authority by allowing the children to play one parent against the other. The child learns that "might makes right." When his parents ignore one day what they punish the next, he feels anxious, never knowing what his limits are.

Mixed messages. A mixed message sends one message on a verbal level and a contradictory message on a nonverbal level. Sarcasm is an example of a message in which the literal content is contradicted by the tone: A child who makes a mistake is told, "That was really bright." Another example of a verbal/behavioral mismatch is a parent who promises to spend time with a child, but then makes other plans or is bored or preoccupied during the time they spend together.

Children are confused by mixed messages. It is difficult for them to make sense of the contradiction. They tend to believe the nonverbal or behavioral message over the verbal one. If they comment on the discrepancy, they may be told that they are crazy or that they are imagining things. Thus a child comes to question the truth of his own feelings, needs, and perceptions.

Chaotic. The family may be disorganized and unreliable, with no set schedules for shopping, meals, or transportation: Members miss appointments; they are late for work and for school; parents don't provide adequate food or clothing. Parents may disappear on drunken binges or after fights without saying when they will be back, forcing their children to fend for themselves. Just as suddenly, they reappear without explanation.

The child learns that he can't count on his family and that he can't expect to get what he needs. He assumes that he will have to provide for himself, even when he's too young to do an adequate job. He then blames himself for his failure.

Rigid. The family may be authoritarian, with strict rules that don't take feelings into account or schedules that provide little leeway for spontaneity. Some parents subscribe to dogmatic religious or political beliefs that dictate much of what family members are supposed to think or feel. Children are likely to be punished for expressing contrary opinions. A gay son may learn to fear homosexuality, associating it with sin, sickness, and disgust, condemning himself for his forbidden feelings.

Isolated. The family is often a closed system. Members keep to themselves, with few friends or outside contacts. Children are discouraged from associating with neighbors or bringing friends home to play. A gay son has little access to other adults who are more open in their opinions. He has no one to talk to about his thoughts or feelings. He assumes that it's dangerous to open up to anyone and believes that he's the only one who has same-sex attractions.

Secretive. Nobody says anything to teachers, neighbors, or friends about abusive interactions among family members. All family matters are kept private; any violation of this rule is considered a betrayal. Within the family, there may be secrets that some members know about but which are never openly acknowledged: children from a previous marriage, adoption, pregnancy, serious illness, substance abuse, or incest. These secrets continue to influence and distort the family's interactions. Sexual orientation is another secret that no one acknowledges or discusses. A gay youth may remain unaware of gay relatives who could provide support.

Lack of communication. There is little honest communication within the family. Parents rarely listen, frequently interrupt, and talk behind each other's back. They do not acknowledge conflict or try to negotiate mutually acceptable solutions. A gay youth realizes that he is not likely to be heard with any concern or empathy, so he keeps his confusion, self-condemnation, and sexual feelings to himself.

Suppression of feelings. Children are expected to be "seen but not heard." Instead of eliciting feelings, parents tell their children what they are supposed to think and feel. They are punished for "talking back" or expressing anger because it is "disrespectful." They are told to "count their blessings" when they feel sad or they are "given something to cry about." A gay youth realizes that his own feelings are a source of danger to himself, so he learns to suppress them.

Uncontrolled rage. While the children must suppress their feelings, the parents are free to vent uncontrolled rage. They may smash things, throw pets against the wall, hit each other, and punish the children arbitrarily. A child is naturally frightened by this violence. Nothing he does seems to make a difference in how he is treated, so he feels anxious and insecure. A gay son may fear this violence being turned on him if his sexual orientation is discovered.

Denial of addictive behavior. The parents may deny that they are addicted to alcohol or drugs, even when it's obvious to everyone else. Family members rarely discuss reactions to obviously drunken, violent, or other abusive incidents. After fights, everyone ignores the broken windows, holes in the walls, or black eyes. A child learns that substance abuse, violent outbursts, and denial are normal ways to deal with feelings. A gay youth may develop a distorted view of whether intimacy is possible between men if most of his interactions with other males have been abusive.

Scapegoating. Children often are used as scapegoats for the shortcomings of their parents, who displace their anger onto the children regardless of whether they actually did (or failed to do) anything. The parents may accuse their children of being sneaky, unreliable, dishonest, or dirty-minded. A gay youth may assume that his parents have discovered his secret, rather than realize his parents' accusations are a reflection of their own conflicts and unconscious fears.

Children take on adult responsibilities. Parents may act more like siblings than parents by involving the children in their quarrels, confiding in them, and asking for advice. A youth may try to protect his mother from abusive interactions but then bear the brunt of his father's retaliation. He may be used as a substitute mate, both emotionally and incestuously. Children may be expected to take on the task of caring for siblings who aren't much younger than themselves. By growing up too soon, a child misses out on his own childhood. He learns to adapt to others' needs and to disregard his own.

Children develop symptoms to protect their parents. Many children become so sensitive to their parents' conflicts that they develop symptoms to keep their parents' marriage from falling apart. Some of these symptoms include bed-wetting, stealing, lying, hyperactivity, doing poorly in school, and getting into fights. The parents may become preoccupied with their "problem child," never realizing how the child's symptoms result from their own unresolved disputes.

The Intergenerational Cycle

Some dysfunctional parents suffer from unresolved rage from their own abusive childhood. If they were never allowed to express disappointment to their parents, for example, their child's disappointment may reawaken emotions that they had suppressed in response to their parents' rigidity. Unless they can work through the effects of their early abuse, it is unlikely that they will be able to tolerate the expression of strong emotions by their children. Instead of empathizing with their child, they punish him for expressing sadness, fear, or frustration.

If his parents cannot tolerate his emotions, a child feels anxious. He learns to suppress his feelings to take care of his parents. Instead of being soothed and comforted by the adults in his life, he becomes a nurturing parent for them. His parents are thus relieved from having to examine how their own unresolved feelings and conflicts have led them to suppress their child's emotions.

As an adult, he will tend to look toward his own children (or partner) for the acceptance he never received from his parents. But because his feelings were not accepted when he was a child, he may find it difficult to tolerate the expression of strong emotions in others. He may also pick a partner who, like his parents, is incapable of empathizing with him. The cycle of discounting and evading feelings continues in a dysfunctional relationship.

The way out of this cycle is for a man to recognize the feelings and reactions he had in response to his family. As he allows himself to feel his emotions, he is more likely to tolerate emotional expression by others without feeling anxious or blamed, because he is already in touch with his own emotional life. Others, in turn, can listen to him without feeling threatened, which replaces the abusive cycle with a positive cycle of empathic understanding.

Types of Abuse

Just because a child is unhappy or feels mistreated doesn't necessarily mean he is being abused. Yet much of what is called "discipline" in child-rearing contains an unnecessary level of cruelty.[3] Survivors of childhood abuse grow up with the assumption that abusive treatment is normal, so they are often confused about whether they were abused. In this section, we will take a look at how to distinguish abusive treatment from appropriate limit-setting, and then describe four common types of abuse.

The testing of rules is a natural phase in child development: A child needs to explore the limits of his independence. If his parents feel comfortable with his exploration, they can enforce limits that are appropriate for his age and true capabilities, yet encourage him to grow beyond these limits when he is ready to handle the next level of responsibility.

The ability to tolerate delayed gratification takes time to develop. Children often cry when they don't get their way. Parents may feel guilty and angry when their child is upset. If they experience his distress as a comment on their own inadequacy rather than understanding that children often feel frustrated, they may vacillate between trying to satisfy his desires, talking him out of his unhappiness, or telling him that "big boys don't cry." They may assume that listening to feelings leads to giving in to a child's demands. They don't realize that they can acknowledge his frustration and still maintain appropriate limits. A child needs firm and consistent limits set on behaviors that are inconsiderate to others or dangerous to himself. He also needs parents who can acknowledge his disappointment without feeling threatened by his feelings.

Parents' lack of knowledge about child development and their own unresolved conflicts can lead to abusive interactions. Abuse cuts across all class and ethnic lines. Listed below are four common forms of child abuse.

Emotional Abuse

Emotional abuse includes put-downs, sarcasm, and name-calling. Telling a child repeatedly that he's never going to amount to anything, that he's a liar and a sneak, or that he ought to be ashamed of himself can result in a self-fulfilling prophecy: He assumes that he is incompetent, so what's the use in trying? No one trusts him anyway, so why not lie? If he's shameful, why not do shameful things?

Emotional abuse can also take more subtle forms. A child may be arbitrarily excluded from family events or outings, or be restricted from favorite activities. Ridicule or punishment for expressing feelings is also a form of emotional abuse. Suppressing feelings interferes with a child's ability to heal from emotional distress and can contribute to post-traumatic symptoms.

In more severe cases, emotional abuse can take the form of degrading and humiliating punishments, such as a boy being forced to wear a diaper in public for wetting his bed; solitary confinement for extended periods; humiliation for masturbating and staining his sheets; and psychological terror, such as destroying favorite toys, threats of violence, or torturing pets.

It's possible to set appropriate limits without being abusive. *Children do not need to be hit or humiliated to be properly disciplined.*[4]

Physical Abuse

Many parents still subscribe to the notion of "spare the rod and spoil the child" to defend their use of physical punishment, not realizing that they may be displacing their own anger and frustration onto their children. Child protective services in the United States will usually get involved with cases of corporal punishment only if there are obvious marks left on the body, such as bruises, welts, or wounds. Some countries, such as Sweden, have outlawed corporal punishment not only in schools but in homes, recognizing the harmful effects of violence on a child's development.

Physical abuse can escalate in severity over time. Some parents are especially incensed if their child tries not to cry or show that he's affected by the abuse. More severe physical abuse includes being slapped across the face; lashed with a belt or a stick; punched with a closed fist; and physical torture, such as being tied up, burned, cut, stabbed, or shot.

Sexual Abuse

Sexual abuse includes inappropriate touching and innuendoes, not only from immediate family members but from other relatives, family friends, care givers, or strangers. A child may become a substitute mate for one parent, emotionally as well as sexually. A child may also be used to humiliate the other spouse through sexual comparisons. More severe forms of sexual abuse include fondling of genitals, intercourse, forced oral and anal sex, and ritual abuse. We will go into more detail about the effects of sexual abuse in chapter 3.

Neglect

As mentioned in the section on chaotic families, some parents simply do not provide their children with basic care. They may leave their children unattended, neglect food and clothing, forget to change diapers, ignore dental and medical care, and be unavailable for emergencies. Some kids are never registered for school, while some are abandoned altogether.

Another form of neglect is emotional abandonment. The parents are so preoccupied with overwork, illness, alcoholism, or depression that they are rarely available to attend to their children's needs for nurturing, love, empathy, and acceptance.

Even subtle forms of abuse can have damaging effects on a child's self-esteem. Someone who comes from an extremely chaotic family may be able to identify the obvious dysfunction in his upbringing and learn how to protect himself from assault, whereas a boy whose confidence was subtly undermined by a father who implied that he was never going to get anywhere might internalize this conclusion. He will have a difficult time seeing how this might have been a reflection of his father's inadequacy or envy, rather than a true measure of his own capabilities.

The Particular Abuse of Gay Boys

A heterosexual child is just as likely to grow up in a dysfunctional family as a gay child. However, many of the above traits may be exacerbated for a gay youth, especially if he doesn't conform to stereotypical masculine roles.

A dysfunctional family is especially likely to reflect and reinforce the homophobic attitudes of the surrounding culture. A gay youth may feel guilty and confused about his attractions, but he can't confide his true feelings to anyone without becoming the target of emotional, physical, or sexual harassment. He learns very early to suppress his feelings toward other males and may develop a secret life apart from his family.

A father may be overly invested in his son's involvement in Little League, Boy Scouts, or other traditionally male activities that encourage competition with other boys. If the boy isn't interested, he may be ridiculed for never doing well enough, and then feel guilty for disappointing his father. His father's withdrawal may be experienced as emotional abandonment. The boy tends to blame himself for his father's disdain or unavailability, instead of realizing that his abandonment is due to his father's own limitations.

Physical education classes often embrace military-style training that is hypermasculine and degrading to sensitive boys. Fear of being sexually aroused in the locker room leads many boys to avoid these classes altogether. Some gay men associate physical fitness with this hostile environment. Later on, they may reject physical exertion altogether or overidentify with an exaggerated image of masculinity in the gym.

Growing up gay in a homophobic culture can be very similar to growing up in a dysfunctional family, even without especially abusive parents, because of the secretiveness, shame, and self-blame associated with homosexuality. In most families, no one even considers the possibility that a child might be gay. This heterosexual bias makes it unlikely that a gay youth would reach out to his parents when he feels confused about his sexual orientation. Without a trusted adult to turn to, he may suppress his feelings and try to change, then blame himself for his failure to do so. The lack of parental understanding encountered by so many gay youths resembles the emotional neglect of abusive families. A gay youth's parents may not be purposely abusive or even homophobic, but few parents discuss homosexuality in an open or accepting manner. Their son has no way of knowing that they might be willing to hear about his struggle. They remain oblivious to his turmoil, and he has to do the best he can to come to terms with his sexual orientation in emotional isolation.

Relating These Ideas to Your Own Experience

- How did your parents meet your needs for nurturing, love, empathy, and acceptance?
- Which of the dysfunctional traits listed above can you identify in your own family?
- How did your family exhibit these traits?
- How were your parents reared by your grandparents?
- Can you see ways in which your parents are caught in an intergenerational cycle? How has this affected you?
- Can you identify ways in which you were abused or neglected?
- What was your experience like growing up gay in your family?
- Do you recall being abused for being gay, or for not conforming to male role expectations?
- If your family was functional in most respects, how did your realization that you were gay affect your interactions with your family?

3

▼

Effects of Abuse on
Gay Sexuality

Many boys are sexually abused through incest, molestation, and sexual assault.[1] *The emotional climate of terror toward same-sex attractions is also a form of sexual abuse.* Even if we have never been molested or raped, many of us have been harassed or have anticipated assault simply because of our sexual orientation. This chapter will look at the effects of such abuse on gay male sexuality.

The topic of sexual abuse touches on sensitive issues within the gay community. Some gay men question the homophobic assumptions that underlie much of the media's coverage of child molestation. Men who were molested as children often feel invalidated when the trauma they have experienced is minimized. Our society tends to deny adolescent sexuality and pretends that gay youths don't exist. In the following section, we'll take a look at some of these issues in an attempt to clarify what we mean by sexual abuse.

Child Molestation and Homophobia

Concern about child sexual abuse has been exploited by some religious and political groups to deny civil rights to gays. They equate homosexuality with child molestation and accuse us of trying to "recruit" or "entice" young people into a "homosexual lifestyle." Although the fear of sexual molestation frequently has been used to perpetuate homophobic attitudes, most men who molest boys don't consider themselves gay. They are not attracted to the secondary sex characteristics of adult males, such as body hair and beards. They tend to be sexually fixated on prepubescent children and molest both girls and boys.[2]

Many child molesters were themselves sexually abused as children, but this doesn't mean that if you were sexually abused you are likely to become an abuser yourself. Only a small percentage of those who were sexually abused go on to molest children as adults. A man who has worked through the trauma of early abuse is much less likely to become a perpetrator. He has a clear understanding of the effects of the abuse on his own childhood and would never want to harm another child in the same way he was harmed.

Age of Consent and
Youthful Curiosity

The power imbalance between adults and children makes it difficult for a child to refuse an adult's sexual request. Children should be free to explore their sexuality at an age-appropriate time with peers and not be pressured into sexual contact by adults.

Heterosexual youths are generally expected to begin their sexual exploration during adolescence. They have school dances, clubs, and youth groups in which to practice social and dating skills. Their sexual interests are reflected in the media and approved of by their own families, who encourage dating and courtship.

In contrast, most young gays have little access to accurate information about homosexuality and are afraid to discuss their attractions with peers. Because of the danger of admitting their true attractions to other teenagers, gay youths often have sex with older men. Some gay men remember these contacts as pleasant or exciting, while others report being scared, confused, and unsure of what was going on. Whether these initial encounters are experienced as having been welcome or traumatic usually depends on the amount of control the youth felt he had over the interaction.

A teenager who seeks sexual contacts in parks or bathrooms is likely to meet men in furtive encounters that provide little opportunity for acknowledging feelings. Instead of dating and getting to know other boys, he may develop a pattern of seeking anonymous sexual outlets disconnected from emotional intimacy. This can distort a young man's sexual and emotional development by focusing all of his needs for intimate contact onto brief sexual encounters. The potential for unsafe sex is high because gay youths are often inexperienced and unassertive. They may not have much information about AIDS, and they rarely have anyone to talk to about how they feel.

The question of whether gay adolescents can give informed consent in a sex-negative and homophobic culture is controversial. Some gay men assume that sex with older men is a rite of passage for gay youths, while others see it as potentially harmful. This controversy is reflected in the wide variation in age-of-consent laws.[3] It's normal for gay teenagers to have fantasies about older men, but actually having sex with an older man can be very confusing because of the power imbalance between teenagers and adults in our culture. Sexual relationships between men and youths can also become exploitive if the adult is in a position of authority, or when money, drugs, food, housing, and other survival needs are exchanged for sexual favors.

Homophobic attitudes set the scene for exploitation by isolating gay youths from their peers. Casual sex with older men will probably continue to be a common sexual outlet for gay youths in our culture as long as so few opportunities exist for them to meet and openly date other young men.

A Definition of Sexual Abuse

The following description is not a legal definition, nor does it cover all the possible ways in which a boy might feel sexually abused. It is an attempt to identify a range of potentially exploitive experiences. Sexual abuse can be subtle. Some of these examples may not be sexually abusive in and of themselves, but they might be experienced as abusive if coercion is involved. These descriptions may evoke feelings or memories that will help you assess your own reaction to early sexual encounters.

Sexual harassment. Sexual harassment consists of comments, innuendoes, or looks that embarrass, humiliate, or coerce a boy sexually. These might include making personal comments about his sexual development; staring at him while he is using the toilet; spying on him while he is dressing, taking a shower, or masturbating; showing or taking sexual photographs; or exposing oneself to him.

Unwanted sexual contact. Sexual contact includes oral, anal, and genital intercourse; fondling of nipples, buttocks, and genitals; other erotic touching, such as a tongue in one's ear, being stroked along the thigh, and deep kissing. It can also include touching that wouldn't appear erotic to an outward observer, such as tickling, wrestling, or other rough play, but which is being used as a cover for sexual contact. If your uncle tickled and wrestled with you when you were a boy, it doesn't necessarily mean he was being sexual. Boys commonly enjoy rough-housing with their brothers, fathers, and other men. You need to judge for yourself whether this kind of play felt sexual or coercive. Some physical abuse may also have a sexual component to it, such as requiring a boy to pull his pants down or strip before he is spanked or lashed with a belt.

Sex with a person who is unable to give informed consent. Persons who are unable to give informed consent include children and anyone who is unconscious or severely intoxicated.

Sex with someone who is in a subordinate position. Subordinate positions include younger siblings, psychotherapy clients, physicians' patients, office subordinates, students, and dependent youth (such as youth who are in foster care, group homes, juvenile detention, or out on the street).

Types of Sexual Abuse

Below are descriptions of several types of sexual abuse, all of which can interfere with the formation of a healthy gay identity.

Incest

Incest means sexual contact between family members, but in recent years the term has been broadened to include sexual contact between a child and any trusted, known adult or adolescent with whom the child has ongoing contact, such as a stepparent, neighbor, coach, clergy, or family friend.

Incest is a taboo in almost every culture.[4] Prohibiting intercourse between family members makes sense genetically, but it also makes sense socially, because of the difference in power between children and adults or older siblings. Yet the taboo seems to be more successful in keeping people from talking about incest than in actually preventing it. Freud steered away from his original findings about incest because he couldn't believe that it was as prevalent as his patients reported.[5]

Child molesters ignore the real developmental differences that exist between prepubescent children and adults. They tend to see a child as seductive or to see themselves as childlike. They rationalize the sexual use of children by claiming that the child wanted the contact. A perpetrator may try to convince a boy that he is doing him a favor by teaching him about sex or that he is doing it because he loves him.

Children rarely question whether adults have the right to impose their will upon them. A boy who has been physically or emotionally abused by other family members may be particularly vulnerable to the attention he receives from a trusted adult. He may feel special sharing a secret with one of the few adults who seems to care about him. His need for attention from adults becomes confused with satisfying the sexual desire of the abuser. He may realize that something isn't right because the perpetrator insists that they keep their contact a secret, threatening exposure or physical harm if he tells anyone.

Not all sexual abuse of boys is by men; some women abuse children, too. Sexual advances by a woman can be very confusing for a boy who has been taught that he should be ready and willing for any sexual adventure. The media reinforce the notion that a boy who has sex with a woman is lucky. As an adult, other men may kid him about "getting some early." If the abuse was by the boy's mother, he may feel deeply conflicted by the experience. He may believe that he was responsible for initiating the contact. He may blame himself for becoming aroused or feel ashamed if he wasn't able to perform. Feelings of longing may be mixed with intense guilt and the impulse to punish himself.

Not all sexual abuse by women involves sexual intercourse or direct fondling of genitals. A mother may insist on bathing a boy even after he's able to bathe himself. She may ask him for back rubs after a bath, or massage his chest when he goes to bed until he becomes aroused. She may indulge in prolonged kisses or embraces.

The concept of emotional incest has been developed to describe a mother who looks to her son to satisfy the emotional needs that are not being met by her husband. She may dote on the boy, make comments about his physical development, and become jealous of the time that he spends with his friends. She may confide in him about her disappointment with his father or disclose other deep-seated conflicts. Rather than seek help from other adults, she looks to her son for comfort. Not every mother who confides in her son is being emotionally incestuous, but a mother who consistently expects her son to fill the place of an adult mate can interfere with his sexual and emotional development.

Many men who were sexually abused as children by their fathers or stepfathers feel a great deal of anger toward mothers who did not protect them. They see the perpetrator as sick, but cannot understand how their mothers could have allowed the abuse to continue. Some mothers may not have known that it was going on. Others may not have wanted to believe it could be true, so they missed obvious cues. Some were themselves abused as children or were battered wives who were afraid to stand up to their husbands. Certainly some women are responsible for not stopping their sons' abuse, and it is understandable that he would feel angry. It may be easier for him to feel angry toward his mother than toward his father because he feels less physically threatened by her. Men are socialized so strongly to be independent that they may resent the dependency they had on their mothers and feel betrayed by their mothers' lack of protection. Mothers and other women often take the brunt of male survivors' anger, even though it might be more effectively directed toward the men who perpetrated their abuse.

Molestation by Strangers

Molestation by strangers is not as common as incest, although it receives more attention from the press, probably because of our cultural denial of incest. A child is three times more likely to be molested by a recognized, trusted adult than by a stranger.[6]

However, sexual abuse by strangers also occurs. It may be more coercive than incest and leave lasting scars because of the fear and physical threat involved. A boy may be too ashamed to reveal what happened to him out of fear that others will suspect he is gay. Such a secret is a tremendous burden and can cause a great deal of anxiety. If he can tell his parents what happened and be believed and comforted, the traumatic effects may not be as severe or as long-lasting as they are likely to be if he has to keep the abuse secret.

Sexual Harassment and Assault

Another form of sexual abuse toward gay boys is sexual harassment and assault by peers. Taunts, gay-bashing, and shunning all serve to reinforce straight-male role values. A boy who becomes aroused in the locker room, expresses affection toward other boys, or exhibits any other gender role nonconformity, is likely to be attacked or humiliated.

Sexual harassment in the workplace includes homophobic comments and discrimination and the expectation of sex for favorable evaluations, promotions, or even for employment itself. Homophobia also can take more subtle forms: being passed over for promotion or being invited without your partner to office parties or family gatherings.

Homophobic assault does not end when we reach adulthood. Violence against gays or men perceived as gay is a constant threat even in the gay neighborhoods of large cities. Having to scan the environment for potential danger is an unremitting source of trauma for gay men. In addition to physical injury, street attacks often result in long-lasting post-traumatic symptoms, such as anxiety, depression, self-blame, and rage.

Forced Sex and Rape

The term "homosexual rape" means same-sex rape, yet it carries the connotation that the rapist is gay. Rape by strangers, rape in prison, and rape in the military are usually perpetrated by heterosexual men.[7] Forced oral sex and anal rape are underreported because men assume they should be able to protect themselves. If they report that they weren't able to stop the assault, they are often blamed for it, just as women are.

Date rape between gay men also occurs, although it is even less frequently reported than rape by strangers. A gay man may assume that he brought the rape on himself through his own ambivalence, through missing cues, or by not being assertive enough. He may have a difficult time admitting to himself that he was assaulted. The law has only recently recognized that a woman has the right to refuse sexual advances by any man (including her husband) even if she invites him home. Gay men also have the right to refuse any sexual act and to insist on safer sex. Both partners should be free to change their minds and say "no" at any point during sexual contact.

Attempted rape and threats of assault can be just as traumatic as being actually raped or beaten, but sometimes a gay man who is able to stop an assault is treated as if nothing really happened. He may feel more empowered if he was able to prevent the rape or escape assault, but the source of trauma is very similar: The unexpected violation of trust and safety, the potential loss of control, and the sense of fear and endangerment are also present during attempted assaults of any kind. These attempts can lead to post-traumatic effects, such as flashbacks, nightmares, and hypervigilance, similar to the symptoms experienced by men who are actually raped or attacked.

Ritual Abuse and Pornography Rings

Cult-related sexual abuse involves severe sexual degradation, injury, and even murder.[8] Some cults include child pornography rings and child slavery. Boys who have been kidnapped, held captive, and forced to participate in these activities are often brainwashed, believing that they will be killed if they ever tell anyone what happened to them. Ritual survivors may develop severe post-traumatic stress symptoms such as multiple personalities to distance themselves from the terror of these experiences. Some may engage in self-mutilation (see the section on self-mutilation below). They need specialized help to come to terms with this devastating trauma (see resources for ritual abuse survivors in appendix II).

Street Hustling

Some boys are forced out of their home when their parents find out that they are gay, or they run away to avoid an abusive environment. With few resources, many boys fall into the hustling scene in big cities. Runaways and other boys from abusive families are especially vulnerable to solicitation on the street. Although most male hustlers work on their own, a few boys are forced into prostitution rings, where they are kept as virtual slaves. Their pimps have them followed and punish them if they try to run away or keep money for themselves. Many hustlers become addicted to hard drugs and become entangled in drug deals involving massive amounts of money. They blow the money and then get beaten or killed when the dealer comes looking for them.

Some hustlers wear flashy clothes and brag about their sexual attraction, using sex to boost their self-esteem and to feel in control.

While they may find the money and attention initially gratifying, over the long run the hustling scene tends to perpetuate a negative self-image.

A substantial number of hustlers were sexually abused as children.[9] They often learn to dissociate from their feelings during sexual contact. They may see themselves as a commodity and believe that being used is all they're good for. They expect that adults are only interested in them for sex and may find men who will take care of them in exchange for sexual favors.

A man might genuinely want to help a hustler get off the street, but may also be interested in him sexually. This creates a dual role: He is supporting the young man as well as becoming his sexual partner. An exchange of sex for survival needs can replicate the boy's earlier abuse. This dual role creates an arrangement in which the boy is still prostituting himself rather than being loved for who he is. The hustler may feel grateful at first for a place to live, but eventually he may also come to resent the man who took him in.

Homeless youths and street hustlers shouldn't be taken advantage of simply because they appear to be "wise to the scene." They need a home where their survival does not depend on their willingness to engage in sex. The prostitution of adolescents is a form of sexual abuse which lowers their self-esteem and contributes to self-destructive behavior. A clear separation must be made between the roles of parent/protector and potential sexual partner to prevent further exploitation.

Adults who advertise sexual services in gay newspapers may not see themselves as exploited, but young street hustlers who have been sexually abused often fall into prostitution as a reaction to early trauma. Although some young men brag about their work, this cavalier attitude may be a cover for deep-seated conflicts. As they grow older, many hustlers get in touch with memories that link their prostitution with earlier sexual abuse.

Abuse by Helping Professionals

Psychotherapists and other helping professionals can play an important role in recovery from incest and other childhood sexual abuse. Clients often feel grateful, admiring, and even attracted to their therapists. These are natural feelings, and there is nothing wrong with having a crush on your therapist. However, these feelings should be discussed within the therapeutic framework and not acted on.

Sexual contact with clients is prohibited by the code of ethics in every psychotherapy profession (and by law, in some states). Even if clients express sexual interest, therapists know that it's their responsibility to maintain a professional relationship. It can be very traumatic for an incest survivor (or any other therapy client) to have a relationship of trust violated once again by a person in such a sensitive position of authority.[10]

Reactions to Sexual Abuse

Little media attention has focused on the sexual abuse of boys, so male incest survivors usually feel very isolated. As more men share their experiences, however, it's clear that sexual abuse has had a profound impact on their sexual development and later intimate relationships, similar to the effects experienced by women sexual abuse survivors.[11]

When men make the connection between current symptoms and early abuse, they may feel a profound sense of loss and be outraged that they were so adversely affected by the people who were supposed to have loved and protected them. Yet they often feel relieved to know that these effects are common symptoms of sexual trauma—they aren't exaggerating or overreacting, and it's not their fault that they were affected by the abuse.

In addition to the effects listed below, sexual abuse survivors may experience post-traumatic symptoms common to other forms of child abuse (see chapter 4). Appendix I includes a detailed list of effects described by men who were sexually abused as children. Everyone reacts to trauma in his own unique way. You can look through these sections and see whether these effects match your experience.[12]

The Source of Trauma

Men are socialized to see sex as being compelling and alluring, so it may be difficult to understand how any sexual contact could be as traumatic as sexual abuse is. It's not easy for men to admit that they've been victimized sexually.

The trauma of sexual abuse is caused by the violation of trust by an adult who takes advantage of a child for his or her own purposes. The person who is supposed to be looking out for a boy's best interests ends up exploiting him. It may be flattering for a boy to receive sexual attention from an adult or an older teenager with whom he has a close relationship. It may be difficult for a boy to recognize the exploitive nature of an older person's sexual interest in him. Even when he is grown, he may still have mixed feelings toward the person who abused him and tend to deny that their sexual contact was abusive. He thus blames himself for whatever difficulties he has with sexuality and intimacy as a result of the abuse.

A man who has been sexually abused may associate any touching with sex, which limits his ability to express nonsexual affection. He may believe that his only value is sexual, which leads him to sexualize most of his relationships. When he is rejected sexually, he feels worthless, but when someone has sex with him, he is confirmed in the belief that sex was all that person was interested in from the beginning. Thus it is difficult for him to believe that anyone could love him for who he is.

Uncertain Memories and Denial

Men who were sexually abused as children may come into therapy with post-traumatic complaints, such as lack of intimacy, sexual compulsion, or sleepless nights. They may not at first associate these symptoms with sexual abuse. All they know is that their life isn't going well. During the course of therapy, they gradually uncover memories of early sexual trauma. This often comes as a surprise, accompanied by doubt and confusion.

Survivors tend to discount vague memories, minimize the abuse, and deny that anything really happened. They may offer excuses for the abuser: He was under a lot of pressure, his father was abusive to him, or he was an alcoholic. Part of this denial comes from not wanting to think of themselves as being victims or survivors of incest. They may feel a deep sense of shame, even though it wasn't their fault that they were abused.

Vague memories and denial can also be understood as a form of self-protection. If the abuse involved threats or physical injury, it may have been so traumatic that the child was overwhelmed and avoided feeling the terror of the abuse by dissociating during the assault. Some survivors describe "out of body" experiences in which they watched the whole thing as if it were happening to someone else; or they retreated into what they describe as a very small compartment deep inside where no one could reach them. Others recall feeling numb or shutting down. Some felt as though their body wasn't really theirs and still have a hard time feeling physical sensations.

You may feel frustrated by blocked memories. Be gentle with yourself. Memories of abusive situations will begin to emerge when you are ready to deal with them. You may have body memories of physical sensations, emotional memories of feelings, and you may recall sounds, voices, or smells before you regain visual memories of the actual abuse.

You may need some time away from an abusive family to feel safe enough to tolerate the emergence of intense emotions. It's important to develop a nurturing support system in which your feelings and memories will be respected and believed. This sense of safety and trust can be established in an incest survivors' group or with a psychotherapist who is familiar with sexual abuse. If it has been difficult for you to talk about the abuse, or if no one has ever wanted to listen to your story, it may take a while for you to feel comfortable enough to say what happened to you even in psychotherapy. Part of the healing process is proceeding at your own pace, so that you have control over your disclosure. As you develop trust in a safe and nurturing environment, feelings and memories become more accessible. It can be a relief to tell your story to someone who understands what you have been through.

Self-Blame

Perpetrators commonly try to convince a boy that their sexual conduct is a secret rite of passage that every boy has to experience. A gay youth may assume that he was responsible for the abuse because of his own sexual curiosity. He may feel guilty for having enjoyed certain aspects of the contact. Sexual organs are designed to respond to physical stimulation. It's quite possible to have an erection and ejaculate even if the contact was forced or feels emotionally uncomfortable. Just because the boy was sexually aroused doesn't mean that he wasn't abused.

Children who seek sexual contact with adults should not be blamed for their own molestation. Children often behave seductively at age three or four, and again at puberty. This is part of children's normal developmental growth as they test their limits and powers. Even if a child seems to behave in a seductive manner, however, it is up to the adult to set appropriate limits. Boys who have been sexually abused may seek sex with men as a way of gaining approval and acknowledgment.[13] Because of previous abuse, they confuse sex with their desire for nurturing. They don't have the social skills to ask for what they truly need. Some of the men I have worked with realized that what they really wanted was some attention from an understanding adult, not sex. Even though they may have initiated the contact, they wished that the man had talked with them about their feelings instead of having sex with them.

A perpetrator may convince a boy that he will cause a divorce or other disruption of the family if he reports the abuse. Because of the secrecy and shame associated with the contact, the boy doesn't tell. In the hope of protecting his siblings from abuse, he may offer himself as a sacrifice, not realizing that they are all being abused. Some children are threatened with violence if they tell, and some are physically abused as well.

It's usually only as an adult that a man can see how he might have been able to stop the abuse by threatening to tell or by running away. He may have some illusions about how much control he actually had as a child and feel angry with himself for not being able to stop the abuse or for going along with it. He may blame himself for returning for more, not realizing that his need for a nurturing adult had been sexualized by the abuse. He may also blame himself for not seeing through the lies, threats, and manipulations that the abuser concocted to extort his participation.

There are many reasons why a child may not be able to stop the abuse.[14] He may fear retaliation and feel powerless to confront an adult. There may be no one he can talk to who will believe him, or if he tries to tell he may be blamed for being queer and be accused of bringing the abuse on himself. He may be terrified that he will be killed if he tells anyone, or worried that his family will fall apart. *It's not a child's fault that he isn't able to stop the abuse.* If you were sexually abused as a child, don't blame yourself for not being able to escape or to tell someone. You did the best you could to survive, with limited knowledge and resources.

Confusion over Sexual Orientation

A boy who is molested by a man may become confused about his sexual orientation. Since the offender may have tried to convince him that he really wanted the contact, he may wonder if the abuse influenced his desire for men. He may deny same-sex attractions by trying to prove he is heterosexual. A boy who is molested by a woman may also wonder whether he was turned off to women as a result of this experience.

From my own work, from talking with other therapists, and from the literature, it seems that a higher percentage of gay men than heterosexual men *report* having been sexually abused.[15] This statistic may be the result of a limited, self-selected sample. More research is needed before we can say that a higher percentage of gay men have been sexually abused. It may be more difficult for straight men to admit to having been abused sexually. If they were abused by a man, they may feel ashamed to admit that they weren't able to protect themselves; if they were abused by a woman, it may be difficult to admit that it was confusing or harmful. Homophobia reinforces the silence of straight and gay boys alike in reaction to sexual abuse.

Even if more gay than straight boys are sexually abused, this does not mean that the abuse *caused* their homosexuality.[16] Some gay boys may be more easily exploited because of their sexual curiosity and lack of opportunity for sexual exploration with peers. Although they may be more vulnerable to sexual abuse because of same-sex attractions, they should not be blamed for their own abuse.

Self-Mutilation

Some survivors self-mutilate by burning, cutting, or hitting them-selves. Self-mutilation may be a way to punish themselves for having been abused or for having felt any pleasure during sexual abuse. It may be an attempt to relive and conquer the sense of defilement they were forced to submit to during ritual abuse. They may also use self-inflicted pain to distract themselves from painful reminders of early trauma. Some survivors dissociate during self-injury and are not aware they are hurting themselves. Others mutilate themselves in a desperate effort to feel *anything*.

A sexual abuse survivor may feel that at least he has more control when he injures himself. As a child, he may have stayed awake at night, anticipating an assault. After he had been molested, he could finally get some rest. This pattern may repeat itself when he is a young adult: He feels restless and anxious until he cuts himself; then he can relax and go to sleep.

Severe sadomasochistic rituals that result in physical injury or degradation can also be a form of self-punishment. If you have been mutilating yourself, or if you lose yourself to the point of injury during sex, you need professional help to learn how to deal with early trauma in a way that allows you to heal instead of continuing to injure your-self.

Disclosing the Abuse

Young children may not have the vocabulary to explain what has happened to them or feel safe enough to tell. Looking back, you may see various ways in which you tried to let people around you know what was going on, even if you weren't able to talk about it directly. Some of these attempts may have included social withdrawal, poor grades, nightmares, phobias, avoidance of the perpetrator, fire-setting, accidents, or physical symptoms such as stomachaches or headaches.

When the initial trauma occurred, there may have been no one to talk to, or no one who recognized what was happening from the non-verbal cues of a small child. Abuse is hurtful in itself, but it is also traumatic to deal with your fear and hurt in isolation. A child cannot tolerate such intense feelings all by himself, so he may bury his feelings until he feels safe enough as an adult to allow them into awareness.

A gay boy may be especially vulnerable to extortion and blackmail. His perpetrator may threaten to expose him as a homosexual if he says anything about the abuse. The boy may have good grounds for fearing that he will get into trouble if he tells: No one will believe him; he might be blamed for it; or people will accuse him of being a queer.

When you first start dealing with sexual abuse in therapy or in a support group, you may want to be selective about who else you tell about the abuse. If you decide to disclose the abuse to friends, you can expect a variety of reactions. Some people will be very supportive, but others may find it hard to believe that an adult could really do such a thing. A few gay friends may claim that they felt fine about their early sexual experiences and wonder why you were so affected by yours. They may not understand much about post-traumatic effects, so they can't comprehend why something that happened to you a long time ago can still affect you.

You may doubt your own memories, blame yourself for still being affected by the abuse, and find it difficult to defend yourself against unsupportive responses. Some friends are well-meaning but ignorant. They may be able to provide an important source of support if they are willing to listen to you and learn something about sexual abuse and post-traumatic stress. You need to decide for yourself how much you want to educate other people about the abuse so that they can, in turn, support you. You don't have to deal with their reactions at the expense of your own healing. This is especially important to remember if you decide to talk with your family or the perpetrator about the abuse (see the section on Confrontation in chapter 12).

Effects on Intimate Relationships

Sexual abuse can have profound effects on intimate relationships. During unwanted sexual experiences, a boy may have learned to disconnect from his emotions and even from his physical sensations. Detaching himself from his partner may become an automatic response to sexual contact. This affects his ability to be emotionally and erotically present during sexual relations as an adult.

You may have a difficult time disclosing the effects of the abuse to a potential partner, fearing incomprehension or rejection. If you are sensitive to certain types of touch or suffer from impotence, you may tend to withdraw from situations that might lead to sexual contact. By withdrawing, you avoid having to explain yourself, but you may feel isolated and lonely.

Although sexual abuse survivors often know they are sexually attractive, they may still have a poor body image. They often feel defiled by the sexual abuse, as if there were something essentially wrong with them. They may know how to get sexual attention, but not the kind of attention they really want, and may vacillate between compulsive sex and withdrawal from all sexual contact.

Trust is a major issue for men who have been sexually abused, especially if the offender was a relative or friend of the family. They may avoid intimacy because they associate sex with exploitation. The "love" they had at one time was so distorted and confused, they may anticipate betrayal or abandonment if they get close to anyone.

If you were sexually abused at night, you may have trouble falling asleep with a partner. Sleep is a very vulnerable time, so you may wake up to a strange noise with a rush of adrenalin. You may be sensitive to a hand passing over your face or to being touched on sensitive parts of your body. Some men have spontaneous memories of earlier traumatic experiences. You may suddenly believe that you are in the previous situation with your actual abuser. You need to remind yourself where you are, who your partner is, and that you can keep yourself safe.

When you enter a relationship, your partner may not know much about these issues. You risk a certain amount of rejection when you disclose sexual difficulties, but this is less likely to happen with someone who cares about you than with a one-night stand. As you get to know each other, you can explore the effects of the abuse on your relationship, gradually increasing your ability to assert your needs and take care of each other. Many survivors find partners who care about them and give them a great deal of support in their recovery.

Feeling self-conscious about your ability to perform can lead to problems in getting or maintaining an erection. If some sexual activities remind you of the abuse, it may be difficult to believe that what you are doing to your partner is truly pleasurable to him. You can let him know before you make love what feels safe and nurturing and what feels uncomfortable. Some men need to find nonsexual ways to express caring and affection for a while, such as a back rub or sleeping together without having sex. Letting your partner know how you are affected by certain kinds of touch obviously requires that both of you communicate your needs very sensitively. With an understanding partner, you can develop feelings of trust and gradually expand areas of sexual lovemaking.

Your partner may not be sure how to respond to your needs or how to support you. He may wonder whether he will be able to satisfy his own sexual desires and emotional needs. Set aside time now and then to talk about your feelings. Your partner may want some outside support for himself during this process. Couples counseling can help you understand each other's needs, give each other support, and still meet each other's desires in your relationship.

Although you may be determined not to let your sexuality be affected by your abuse, you're more likely to reclaim your sexuality by recognizing ways in which you were affected. Along with this recognition, you may get in touch with a great deal of anger and sorrow. As you recover from the effects of your abuse, however, you will increase your capacity for sexual and emotional intimacy with a loving partner.

Relating These Ideas to Your Own Experience

- Do you remember being touched in any way that felt uncomfortable to you as a child?
- If you were sexually abused, who was the first person you tried to tell?
- If you were too young to tell, or if there was no one in whom you could safely confide, can you identify any childhood behavior that might have indicated that you were having a hard time?

- What were your own early same-sex experiences like? Did you feel as though you were in control of what happened to you?
- If you had sex with an adult when you were a teenager, how did you feel about it then? How do you feel about it now? Would you like anything to have been different about those experiences?
- You might want to take a look at the list of effects of childhood sexual abuse in Appendix I. Write down some of the memories and feelings stimulated by this list and share them in therapy or in your support group.
- What forms of sex feel comfortable to you now? How do you let your partner know what you want sexually? Do you tell him, or do you let him know your preferences nonverbally? How well does your sexual communication work for you?

Emotional, physical, and sexual abuse can all have long-lasting effects. In the next chapter, we will look at other post-traumatic effects that may result from childhood abuse and internalized homophobia.

4

▼

Post-Traumatic Stress

When we are children, and even when we are grown, we need adults in our lives who can understand our experiences and empathize with our feelings. We are less likely to be emotionally scarred by traumatic events when we can express ourselves to someone who will listen to our hurt, sorrow, and fear. An understanding and accepting response from their families is precisely what most abused children lack. The caretakers who should be providing a safe haven for a child are the very ones who are abusing him. Far from being able to understand a child's pain, they feel threatened by the expression of feelings and punish the child for feeling bad.

In this chapter, we will see how growing up in an abusive family is like growing up in a war zone; as a result, gay men who were abused as children often suffer from post-traumatic effects as adults. We will look at how AIDS has been an additional source of mass trauma in the gay community, and we'll explore how internalized homophobia is essentially a form of post-traumatic stress.

Effects of Trauma

The concept of post-traumatic stress was developed to explain the symptoms that many soldiers experienced after returning home from combat, especially following the war in Vietnam and the Arab-Israeli conflicts. The term "shell-shocked" was used in World War II to refer to the same effects. Similar symptoms have been described by Holocaust survivors; prisoners of war; people who have been assaulted, raped, tortured, or ritually abused; and survivors of natural catastrophes. Over the last several years, health providers have also recognized post-traumatic symptoms in adult children of abusive families.[1] Emotional, physical, sexual, and ritual abuse can result in severe, long-lasting effects.

What do we mean by post-traumatic stress? "Trauma" is defined in the manual used by psychotherapists for diagnosing mental health problems as a "psychologically distressing event that would evoke significant disturbance in almost anyone."[2] Depending on the nature of the trauma, the stress may be delayed for months or even years after the actual traumatic event. This is because one's natural ability to absorb trauma is overwhelmed, and it takes time to work through the resulting feelings.

Listed below are common symptoms of post-traumatic stress. You can use these descriptions as a guide for gauging effects of abusive interactions in your own family. Having one or even a few of these symptoms doesn't necessarily mean that you were abused or that you are suffering from post-traumatic stress. Everyone "spaces out" once in a while, has an occasional nightmare, has difficulty concentrating under stress, and occasionally feels the need to withdraw from social activities. What distinguishes post-traumatic stress is having a number of symptoms which consistently interfere with your ability to function in your daily life.

If you come from an abusive family (or if you have been assaulted as an adult), it can be reassuring to realize that *these symptoms are a normal response to trauma*—you are not imagining things and you're not crazy for experiencing post-traumatic stress. At the same time, these effects are not permanent. In Part II we will offer a number of resources that will enable you to work through the trauma and recover from its effects.

- Memory loss
- Difficulty in concentrating
- Dissociation
- Intrusive memories
- Dreams and nightmares
- Hypervigilance
- Physical symptoms
- Anxiety around similar events and associations
- Boundary issues
- Mistrust
- Withdrawal
- Low self-esteem

Let's explore these in more detail.

Memory loss. If you were abused as a child, the trauma may have been so overwhelming that you shut off your feelings and forgot the events that surrounded the abuse. This is a self-protective strategy that helped you get by until you could tolerate these feelings as an adult. As a result, your memories may be vague. You may question whether anything really happened that could explain your current symptoms. Even if you remember abusive incidents, you may minimize their severity.

Difficulty in concentrating. After hearing stories about child abuse, memories and feelings may begin to emerge. You may find that you lose track of what you are thinking or what you are going to do next. You may have difficulty reading or expressing your thoughts in writing, which can interfere with studies or work. Your difficulty in thinking clearly may be an unconscious attempt to protect yourself from painful memories.

Dissociation. Dissociation is the process of separating or "dis-associating" yourself from your feelings or experience. Dissociation takes place on a continuum from simple forgetfulness or "spacing out" to complete splits in consciousness, such as multiple personality.[3] Most people experience at least mild forms of dissociation at times, especially in the face of criticism or internal conflict, but abuse survivors often experience more severe and consistent forms of dissociation. Especially when faced with conflict, important decisions, or demands for intimacy, they may feel numb or emotionally distant.

Detaching oneself from physical trauma can be a useful mode of survival as a child. Even as an adult, it can be used as a natural anesthesia if you can learn to control it consciously. The problem for many survivors is that detaching themselves may become an automatic response to feeling *anything*. This can interfere with their ability to deal with conflict or to be emotionally present in intimate relationships. (To become more "grounded" in the present moment, see the Awareness of Feelings Exercise at the end of chapter 9.)

Intrusive memories. As an adult you are more capable of working through the feelings elicited by the abuse, so memories begin to rise to the surface. Memories may be stimulated by reports of child abuse on the news, by hearing other people's stories, or by reading books such as this one. Sudden memories of forgotten incidents are common during psychotherapy for early abuse.

These memories may be disturbing, especially if they bring back incidents that you had forgotten. You may wonder what else might have happened that you haven't remembered yet. Sometimes people feel overwhelmed by the onrush of feelings from long-forgotten incidents, but for the most part memories tend to arise when you are ready to deal with them.

Dreams and nightmares. Memories may also return spontaneously through dreams and nightmares. Although they can feel very uncomfortable, dreams and the recovery of painful memories are part of the natural healing process. Dreams may provide important clues about forgotten abuse. Some dreams replay actual incidents, such as being chased, hit, or sexually abused. Others may symbolize the emotional impact of abusive experiences. For example, you may have a dream about your father threatening to shoot you, even if this never actually happened. The symbolic meaning may be that as a child you felt as if you were in danger of being annihilated when he hit you, sexually abused you, or ridiculed you for not living up to his expectations. As you work through these dreams and incidents, you may find that your nightmares gradually change from your being chased or terrorized to dreams in which you are able to master the conflict: You turn on the monster and wrestle him to the ground; or you disarm your father and tell him that he can no longer threaten you.

Hypervigilance. A survivor of a traumatic incident tends to scan his environment in anticipation of further attacks. It is difficult to relax his guard. He may experience a startle response and a rush of adrenalin to unexpected noises, touches, or other stimuli that remind him of the trauma. He may be a light sleeper and have a difficult time screening out nonthreatening noises.

You can begin to counter this tendency by noticing the rush of adrenalin, recognizing the current stimulus, and identifying the original source. You can remind yourself that you are safe now, and that you can relax. Don't put yourself down for continuing to scan your environment. You learned to be vigilant to survive. It takes a long time for this conscious recognition to influence physical reactions.

Physical symptoms. Survivors of abuse often suffer physical symptoms such as headaches, back problems, and digestive disorders that have no organic cause. These problems may arise from emotional conflicts, but they are real nonetheless—they are not just in your head. You should have them checked by a physician to rule out any underlying diseases. Stress-related symptoms often can be alleviated by learning how to deal with stress in more constructive ways and by working through underlying emotional conflicts.[4]

Anxiety around similar events and associations. Similar to hypervigilance, associations may include smells, sounds, and other sense memories of the abuse. A door opening, a shadow falling across the floor, the smell of after-shave, or even the sound of a car pulling into the driveway can cause anxiety if it was associated with repetitive abusive experiences. Other associations may include criticism, abandonment, sexual advances, or interpersonal conflict. All of these can elicit an anxiety response that seems out of proportion to the stimulus.

If you have no memory of the abusive experience itself, these responses can be disturbing. Instead of criticizing yourself for overreacting, remember that such reactions seldom come out of nowhere. Your anxiety may be a clue to forgotten memories of early abuse.

Boundary issues. Dysfunctional families tend to have a poor sense of boundaries. They may intrude on others' physical space, use their things, and treat another person's body as if they owned it. They may also intrude psychologically by telling a person what he is "really" thinking or feeling. This can lead to gaps in a person's sense of what's appropriate in his relationships with other people. As an adult, he may put up with intrusive and abusive behavior because he doesn't realize that he has a right to his own perceptions and feelings, or even to his own body. To protect himself, a person with poor boundaries may put up walls instead (see the section on boundaries in chapter 12).

Mistrust. A child puts ultimate trust in his caretakers. If this trust is betrayed through abuse or abandonment, his basic sense of safety and security in the world is damaged. He comes to expect others to be untrustworthy and may hesitate to give them a chance to demonstrate their trustworthiness. It's difficult for him to risk becoming close to others because those closest to him were the ones who betrayed his trust in the past. In support groups and through psychotherapy for abuse survivors, he can gradually repair his ability to trust other people.

Withdrawal. The anxiety, mistrust, and intrusiveness experienced by survivors of dysfunctional families may lead to withdrawal from significant social contact. They may lose jobs, isolate themselves, or even neglect personal hygiene. Or they may function from day to day, but feel alienated, bored, and depressed. Without much to look forward to, they find little meaning in their lives.

Low self-esteem. The internalization of abuse leads many people to feel bad about themselves. They don't see much potential for improving their lives, because they blame themselves for having sunk to this level in the first place. Once they realize that their self-blame and negative self-image are reactions to earlier abuse, they begin to understand that they might not always have to feel this way.

Some people experience traumatic events in their lives without suffering severe forms of post-traumatic stress.[5] You shouldn't compare your own emotional injury with that of others, or blame yourself for being affected more or less severely than anyone else.

Even if you understand the source of your post-traumatic symptoms, certain events may still trigger anxiety. However, you will be less likely to blame yourself for experiencing these effects. You will gradually gain confidence that you can work through post-traumatic symptoms and heal from past abuse.

AIDS as a Source of Trauma

AIDS has been a tremendous trauma for the gay community. The loss of thousands of lives has had an enormous impact on all of us, whether or not we are HIV-infected ourselves. By recognizing that AIDS is a source of stress, we can normalize our reactions to the epidemic. We need not experience our feelings and reactions in isolation—we can reach out to others for support. We can see the traumatic impact of AIDS in a number of areas:

Trauma of life-threatening illness. Life-threatening illness is a source of serious trauma. The uncertainty of prognosis can lead to a great deal of anxiety in HIV-infected men, even if they are asymptomatic. Worsening illness may involve the severe alteration or loss of a man's previous abilities and other sources of his identity such as work, body image, sexual interest, and mobility. He may not have much energy to counter these losses and may suffer from depression unless he can develop other sources of self-definition and meaning. These can include his relationship with a loving partner, friendships, involvement in AIDS-related activism, or spiritual beliefs. Some men alter their lifestyles in the hope of boosting their immune system and as a way of reducing their stress.

Hypervigilance. Some men report an increased sensitivity to any sign of illness. A preoccupation with physical symptoms may be a form of hypervigilance. A sore throat, fever, cough, or rash can lead to panic that it might be an AIDS-related condition.

Survivor guilt. The loss of a man's lover or his closest friends to AIDS may lead to survivor guilt. He may have done all he could to assist his partner in keeping well, but he may still imagine that there must have been something more he could have done. He may wonder why he survives when others have died. Survival can also stir up feelings about being emotionally abandoned as a child. If a man blamed himself for his parents' incapacity for emotional warmth and understanding, he may associate the loss of his partner with this abandonment. On an unconscious level, he may assume that if he had been a better companion, his lover would not have left him by dying.

Effects on sexuality. Men who are HIV-positive may fear infecting others, even if they practice safer sex. Men who are HIV-negative may also feel a sense of helplessness and depression, whether or not they have suffered personal losses. They may feel isolated and withdrawn and may experience sexual dysfunction. Uninfected men have just as great a need as infected men to talk about the impact of the AIDS epidemic on their lives. Although most gay men know about safer-sex guidelines, some men alternate between withdrawal from sexual contact and practicing unsafe sex. It may be difficult for them to admit that they are having a hard time with safer sex for they may anticipate negative judgment from other gay men. If they aren't able to talk about their sense of failure or shame, they are likely to continue with unsafe sexual behavior.[6]

The impact of catastrophic losses on the gay community. The entire social network of many gay men has been wiped out by AIDS. They may have been so involved with caring for others that they haven't taken much time to get in touch with their own feelings of sadness. Multiple losses can result in anxiety, depression, withdrawal, and difficulty in concentrating. Intrusive memories, dreams, and loss of interest in daily activities are also common reactions to grief. Men who were intimately involved with the death of a loved one may have a difficult time returning to work or pursuing other relationships.

Unresolved grief can also affect professional care givers such as physicians, nurses, and mental health workers, as well as friends. Unexpressed sorrow can lead to dissociation, difficulty in concentrating, short tempers, and a lack of empathy. It may also lead to social withdrawal to protect oneself from further losses.[7]

The stigma of homosexuality has been compounded by the association of AIDS with gay men. Much of the media coverage has implied that gay sexuality is the source of AIDS, not a virus. We have been blamed by fundamentalists for having brought the epidemic on ourselves. AIDS has given the right wing an excuse for another round of gay-bashing from the pulpit, in the press, and on the street. For men suffering from internalized homophobia, the association of homosexuality with a life-threatening illness can easily awaken feelings of shame in response to the epidemic. The stress of self-blame may also interfere with the functioning of the immune system.

Fear of contagion based on ignorance and misinformation has led to homophobic legislation. Education and outreach efforts have been hampered by unrealistic demands for abstinence and sobriety without providing adequate resources for sex-positive education or substance-abuse treatment. The government's lack of commitment to making AIDS a priority has led to a scattered and haphazard approach to drug trials and research. Gay men, women, the poor, and even middle-class working people faced with life-threatening illness are cut off from their insurance or are forced to pay premiums so high that they cannot continue coverage. Patients are dumped from private hospitals into public facilities, which face cutbacks from state and federal funding. Although it is not the cause of the current crisis in health care, the AIDS epidemic has revealed the shortcomings of a system that is incapable of providing a humane response to the needs of its citizens.

Young men who are still struggling with their sexual orientation often feel confused and conflicted when confronted by the AIDS epidemic. Even if they know the basic information about safer sex, they are unlikely to get any support at school for negotiating safer sex with another man. Young men tend to assume that they are invincible, and many still believe that only older gay men become infected. The result of this denial may be a new wave of infection among men in their teens and early twenties. We need to provide practical support to young gay men that both recognizes their need for peer acceptance and enhances their ability to assert themselves.

Many gay men have successfully countered the homophobic attitudes that suggest that AIDS is a punishment from God, or that we somehow deserve it because of our lifestyle. We are all responsible for doing what we can to protect ourselves and others from the spread of AIDS, but no matter how someone contracts HIV, *no one deserves to have AIDS*. Through AIDS service organizations, rap groups, and friendship networks, gay men are talking more about the emotional impact of dealing with AIDS over many years. Understanding our reactions as coping mechanisms in the face of trauma can help us reach out to others. Talking about self-blame and survival guilt can break our isolation and help us maintain safer sexual practices.

Grieving our losses will not undermine our determination to fight this illness. Mobilizing resources, creating systems of support, and harnessing anger can be effective ways to deal with trauma and to counter self-blame. Many gay men have become involved with education, attendant care, and political lobbying for increased access to health care. Gay men and women with AIDS have taken charge of their own treatment. They have educated physicians, met with researchers, and protested the high cost of medication and the slow pace of drug trials. They have joined with other health coalitions to demonstrate the inadequacy of the health-care system in the United States. They have challenged the U.S. government to be more responsive to the catastrophic impact of AIDS on women, minority communities, and Third-World countries. We can continue to press for the recognition that our health is a vital resource that benefits all of society.

Internalized Homophobia as a Form of Post-Traumatic Stress

"Trauma" was defined earlier in this chapter as a "psychologically distressing event that would evoke significant disturbance in almost anyone." Homophobia is a pervasive and constant stressor in the development of many gay men. Most gay youths grow up in a threatening homophobic atmosphere without family or peer support for their feelings. They are frequently victimized with taunting, hazing, and ridicule. Gay men may be physically attacked simply for not conforming to male roles, or they may be ostracized and shunned. The *anticipation* of rejection or assault can also contribute to self-blame and low self-esteem.

Internalized homophobia can be understood as a form of posttraumatic stress. Symptoms such as hypervigilance, anxiety, mistrust, and withdrawal may develop in response to put-downs, discrimination, and assaults. As a result of this external threat, we may assume there is something fundamentally wrong with us simply because we have loving and erotic feelings toward other men.

As an adult, you may experience some post-traumatic symptoms in reaction to the abuse you may have suffered as a gay boy growing up within a dysfunctional or homophobic family. If you were isolated from others who could accept your homosexuality, you had to keep your feelings to yourself. The pain or anxiety you experience now is a sign that you are ready to confront the past. You can reach out for support from people who accept your sexual orientation and who understand the consequences of early abuse.

Relating These Ideas to Your Own Experience

- Which of the post-traumatic effects listed above have you experienced? Can you identify others that aren't listed?
- Are any of your effects related to homophobia? Which stem from other types of abuse?
- How have you been affected by the AIDS epidemic? This is a huge question. It will probably take most of us years to come to terms with the alterations in our lifestyle, the impact on our social networks, the feelings of fear, and the grief for the losses we have experienced. One way to begin addressing this grief is to look at a few of these effects at a time and to get some support by talking about them with other gay men.

- Can you identify ways in which you are still affected by internalized homophobia?
- Imagine how you would feel if you were completely free of any effects of homophobia. What difference would this make in your daily life? With your family? At work? On your vision of the future?

5

Self-Blame and Shame

In this chapter, we will look at the key role that shame plays in causing us to absorb negative messages from our families and to see how abused children tend to blame themselves for their own abuse. We will also explore how shame influences the development of a false self to accommodate our parents' needs or to protect ourselves from low self-esteem.

Guilt and Shame

It's useful to distinguish between guilt and shame. Guilt has to do with judgments about our *behavior*; shame has to do with judgments about our core sense of *self*.[1]

Guilt

Guilt is the feeling of regret or remorse that we feel for not living up to the expectations that we have for ourselves. If our expectations are based on our true values, we can use guilt to motivate constructive changes in our behavior. We can make amends to those whom we have harmed, for example, or try to improve our abilities. Guilt also can result from values or expectations of ourselves that are unrealistic. In such situations, we need to acknowledge our limitations and adjust our expectations. Guilt can be unnecessarily punitive. Just because we make a mistake, we don't have to judge ourselves harshly. Overriding guilt can lead to its deeper, more entrenched corollary: shame.

Shame

Punitive guilt undermines our core sense of self. When you feel humiliated by your imperfections, you develop a sense that *you* are basically flawed, rather than realizing that human beings make mistakes. Shame stops growth, because there is nothing you can do but try to avoid the humiliation. The avoidance of shame may result in the development of a false self (described later in this chapter) or in self-defeating behavior.

Mistakes can be seen as corrective feedback, not as a judgment of our essential worth. Rather than feeling humiliated by our imperfections, we can learn from our mistakes. Instead of condemning ourselves for not being perfect, we can develop a healthy sense of humility.[2] Acknowledging that we are fallible human beings allows us to improve and grow.

Abuse and Self-Blame

When a child makes a mistake in a well-functioning family, his parents identify the problem, point out the consequences of his behavior, and provide a reasonable opportunity for making amends. The erring child isn't afraid that he has lost his parents' love, because they are not personally threatened by his mistakes. By acknowledging his mistake and making amends, the child develops a sense of responsibility toward other people. He is free to learn from his mistakes, because he is not humiliated by them.

In a dysfunctional family, a child's mistake is perceived as a personal affront to the parents, who may punish the child out of proportion to his behavior. They inflict their own feelings of inadequacy on the child by shaming him. Instead of simply recognizing his imperfections, the child assumes that he is fundamentally defective.

This is why an abused child often believes that he deserves to be abused. The alternative, recognizing that his parents are dangerously flawed and unpredictable, is unacceptable to the child, because he relies on his parents for his very survival. It is less anxiety-provoking to assume that he deserved whatever punishment he got than to think that his parents might be abusive. Moreover, if he believes that he was bad, he can maintain the illusion that by trying to be ''good'' he has some control over what his parents do to him.

The shamed child makes no distinction between his self-concept and his behavior. If he makes a mistake, he sees this as proof of his badness, rather than understanding that we all make mistakes. If his parents abandon him, either physically or emotionally, he sees this as proof of his unworthiness, not realizing that he is being mistreated.

This natural tendency toward self-blame is reinforced by parents who convince the child that they wouldn't have punished him if he hadn't been bad. The child isn't able to distinguish between abuse and appropriate limit-setting. He believes that his parents' out-of-control behavior was caused by his own misdeeds. As he grows older, the youth may remember incidents in which he was purposely mischievous, reinforcing his assumption that he deserved to be punished. Every child misbehaves at times. He may need limits and consequences for certain behaviors, but *a child never deserves to be abused.*

This distinction between behavior and self-concept is very important in the development of a healthy sense of self. If you believe that who you are is defined only by what you do, you are very vulnerable to feeling ashamed. Nobody is perfect at doing anything, and to have the expectation that you must be perfect is a setup for feeling humiliated by your very existence. This sense of humiliation is precisely the experience of a young child who is being abused. Instead of allowing him to make mistakes and to learn from them, his parents humiliate him or hit him for making a mess, for crying, or for making demands—in essence, they punish him for being a child. He learns that his emotions are threatening to his parents, and so he feels ashamed for feeling angry, sad, or afraid. He suppresses his feelings to protect his parents and to prevent punishment or abandonment. He manages to survive, but in the meantime he has lost touch with his emotional life.

Homophobia and Shame

How does a sense of shame develop in gay boys? A boy may have a crush on his best friend without realizing that his feelings might be considered homosexual. He hears the words *queer* or *fag* as put-downs before he knows what they mean. When he realizes that these derogatory terms refer to same-sex attractions, he may feel a great deal of conflict over his self-image.

Most boys absorb the message from the surrounding environment that homosexuality is contemptible. Few gay youths feel safe enough to freely admit same-sex attractions to their families, even if their parents are quite supportive in general. If a boy's parents are harsh and punitive, he may anticipate their disapproval and condemn himself.

Isolated from anyone who can let him know that his feelings are all right, he may try to change. Yet his attraction toward other males persists. Unable to change how he feels, he assumes that there is something inherently wrong with him. He may end up feeling ashamed simply for being who he is.

Religious Shame

In the book of Genesis, Adam and Eve were expelled from the Garden of Eden because they ate the fruit of the tree of knowledge of good and evil. This loss of innocence is portrayed in some churches as the original sin that separated us from God. According to Christian theology, the only way we can find our way back to God from our condition of original sin is through the intercession of Christ.

The story of the expulsion from the Garden of Eden associates the awareness of sexuality with a loss of innocence: They covered themselves in the "shame" of their nakedness. In Catholicism and in most Protestant denominations, sex is supposed to be reserved for procreation within marriage. Sex for pleasure or as an expression of romantic love outside of marriage is considered sinful. Homosexual contact, which does not occur within marriage and which doesn't involve procreation, is condemned by many Christian religious authorities. They claim that the path back to God is closed to gays unless we are celibate.

Religious gay people may experience a conflict between their homosexual attractions and church doctrine. Some gay people leave the church because it seems so hostile to homosexual relationships. Others challenge the homophobic assumptions of their congregations because they believe that homosexuality *is* compatible with their religious beliefs. Gay historians have traced the development of antigay attitudes to show that despite certain passages in the Bible, a strong antihomosexual attitude was the result of political developments in the church's history—it was not something Jesus ever commented on, nor was it an obsession of early church leaders.[3]

Many people see common elements in the mystical traditions of all the world's religions.[4] They understand "original sin," or separation from God, as a metaphor for our separation from our true selves. Our "loss of innocence" has to do with the fact that we have a free will to decide between right and wrong. We must take responsibility for our sexual behavior, just as we must for all our actions, but there need not be any contradiction between sexual morality and homosexuality. Gay people are just as capable as anyone else of treating one another with love and respect, in accordance with our own spiritual beliefs.

Some gays have formed their own congregations so they can continue their worship without the sanction of an official church or temple.[5] Others have found individual congregations that are open to gays even if the parent church is not, and some have gotten involved with one of the few denominations that accepts homosexual relationships.[6] Some gay men have developed their own spiritual gatherings to celebrate elements of pre-Christian paganism, Native American religions, shamanism, or Eastern religions.[7]

All of the foregoing are strategies for dealing with religious traditions that are hostile toward homosexuality. We have these choices as adults, but as children it is very difficult to avoid internalizing the homophobic messages that pervade the teachings of most Protestant and Catholic churches.

Some forms of dogmatic religious instruction can be seen as emotional abuse. Children may be constantly threatened with the devil, hellfire, and eternal damnation for the slightest infractions or sins of thought. Strict religious parents may not realize that emotions often pass once they are acknowledged. Sadness is experienced as ungrateful criticism, the expression of anger is seen as insubordination, and any belief that deviates from church dogma is considered heresy. Instead of empathizing with their children, parents may punish them for expressing any emotion that can be construed as opposition to their authority.

The concept of original sin may be used to enforce shame about sexual feelings. A parent who believes that sex is shameful may suppress his own sexuality. Because he hasn't figured out how to use sex in a balanced way in his own life, he tends to see its expression in others as being lascivious. He will shame a child's natural interest in sex because the child's curiosity threatens to awaken his own forbidden impulses. The sad irony of this suppression is that sexual abuse is not uncommon in families with dogmatic religious beliefs and authoritarian child-rearing practices.

This obsession with sexual shame is not limited to rigid families. Sexual shame drives the political agendas of right-wing fundamentalists who are trying to eliminate reproductive choice and prevent civil rights for gay people.

Development of a False Self

A gay boy who is being abused realizes very early that his true feelings are likely to be rejected. When we combine growing up in a dysfunctional family with the homophobia of the surrounding culture, the pressure to conform can be overwhelming. As adults, we can recognize when we are treated unfairly. We can assert our needs or leave a relationship in order to protect ourselves. A child, however, usually remains stuck in a dysfunctional family unless his abuse is so severe that it comes to the attention of child protective services. He has to find some way to deal with the turmoil in his family and the homophobia of his church and school. Isolated from others who might feel similarly, he may develop a "false self" to present to the world.[8] A false self is a strategy for coping with abuse and for avoiding shame. The child develops a mask that hides his genuine feelings, even from himself. This may help him survive in a hostile environment, but it does so at the expense of his own natural growth. This false self may manifest itself in a number of ways:

- Identification with the aggressor
- Reactive rebellion
- Becoming overly adaptive
- Withdrawal and isolation
- Grandiosity and contempt

Identification with the aggressor.[9] Within a dysfunctional family, a child may internalize his parents' values and imitate their violent behavior. He learns very early that it's too dangerous to express his hurt and anger directly to his abuser, so he may take out his frustration on pets or smaller children.

Similarly, a gay youth may become anxious when he sees other boys exhibiting behavior that reminds him of his own repressed feelings. He condemns them for the thoughts and impulses that he is not able to admit to himself. Ridiculing other boys or gay-bashing provides a release for the feelings of hurt and fear that he had to repress to survive the abuse of his own tormentors. Why would he want to identify with the people who are hurting him? Imitating his tormentors protects him from feeling weak and vulnerable. Identifying with the values of the dominant culture is a way for a member of an oppressed group to transform the experience of fear to one of feeling powerful, but he does this at the expense of his own identity and self-esteem.

Reactive rebellion. A youth needs to separate emotionally, physically, and financially from his parents. This separation process involves exploring different values, clothing, music, and lifestyles, often in response to the interests of his peers. If his parents are secure in their own identity, they can set appropriate limits while still allowing him to assume greater freedoms and responsibilities.

Parents who feel threatened by their son's experimentation with new values may try to restrict his emerging interests. Verbal abuse, arbitrary rules, or condemnation of his lifestyle may provoke an active rebellion. This form of rebellion is natural and healthy if it can be channeled into the youth's development. However, unless he is able to enlist some adult support, he may drop out of school, take drugs or abuse alcohol, get in trouble with the law, and become further alienated from the surrounding culture. Instead of asserting his own needs and feelings, he may oppose anything that reminds him of his parents' values. Oppositional behavior for its own sake can lead to self-defeating behavior.

Conformity to peer pressure is a normal phase of identity formation in adolescence, but because of their isolation, few gay youths find a group to identify with. Some may find kids on the fringe to hang out with and create their own flamboyant style, flaunting their differences. They have fun assuming shocking poses and thrive on the alarm and disdain of their classmates. Their humor often combines rebellion and self-deprecation, similar to the humor that develops among ethnic minorities.

Internalized racism, sexism, and homophobia all have in common the incorporation of the surrounding culture's negative beliefs and stereotypes. Imitating straight men's worst fears is an innocent way to vent hostility and camp it up. Some gay youths, however, confuse their burlesque of oppressive caricatures with their own identity. They reinforce one another's stereotypical behavior and have a hard time gauging when it is safe to be authentic with their friends. Rebellion can become a form of false self when it dominates a youth's life and forms the basis for all his actions.

Becoming overly adaptive. A child is highly attuned to his parents' moods and feelings. He may rationalize and repress his emotions to soothe his parents, even if it means distorting his own self-concept. He may try to convince himself that he needn't feel sad or hurt, and he learns how to ignore painful sensations. If his feelings break through, he may feel ashamed of crying and tries not to let anything bother him.

Some children receive a lot of positive attention for their abilities, but only insofar as these satisfy the parents' needs and reflect favorably on them—not as an appreciation for the children's own natural growth. When his self-worth is determined solely by his usefulness to others, a child is likely to suppress any feelings that don't fit the acceptable image. A gay boy may become the "good son" or the overachiever who appears not to have any needs, but whose true feelings may be suppressed. It can take a long time before he realizes how his own needs might have been distorted to conform to his parents' conception of who he should be.

Withdrawal and isolation. A child who is unable to gain his parents' affection through positive means may resort to disruptive behavior, because negative attention is better than no attention. However, if he's told that he never does anything right, and every attempt at contact is rebuffed or punished, he may stop trying and withdraw. A child may find various ways to confirm his parents' low opinion of him by setting unrealistic goals or by giving up, becoming depressed and isolated. He may swear to himself that he will never allow himself to be hurt again, so he won't let anyone get close to him.

Grandiosity and contempt. Grandiosity may result from the lack of an understanding response from a nurturing parent. Contempt of others is really an expression of a person's disdain for himself. Feeling superior is a way to avoid feeling ashamed of his own inadequacies. Devaluation of others also helps him deny his need for other people. Admitting this desire would stir up an awareness of the profound loss he experienced when he was emotionally abandoned by his parents, which he equates with his own inadequacy. Unless he can grieve for this loss, it will be difficult to admit his need for others. He vacillates between contempt and shame: He either devalues others, or he hates himself. To protect himself from self-hatred, he becomes disdainful or contemptuous of others.

Since he cannot tolerate any imperfection in himself without feeling totally humiliated, it's difficult for him to empathize with other people's feelings. Internalized homophobia, rage at how he has been treated, and shame may all be expressed through contempt or disdain for other gay men. Unresolved rage and a lack of empathy inhibit the development of intimacy in his relationships, and this contributes to a feeling of emptiness.

Shame shadows the lives of many gay men, interfering with their ability to connect with other men in intimate relationships. If we are ashamed of our feelings, we may buy into the very prejudice that has oppressed us: We assume that gay men are promiscuous, superficial, self-centered, or incapable of having a lasting relationship. Unless we become conscious of how we have absorbed these negative messages, internalized homophobia can become a self-fulfilling prophecy: We may end up treating one another in the same way we fear being treated ourselves. Insight about internalized homophobia can allow us to understand the strategies we developed to cope with a hostile environment and can help us develop compassion for ourselves and for other gay men. Instead of taking out our anger on one another for how we have been mistreated, we can reach out to others for support.

Many gay men eventually develop the confidence to express their true selves once they acknowledge their same-sex attractions and establish a network of gay friends. We are more likely to get in touch with our feelings within a supportive community that understands our experience. This support can release us from the self-blame and shame that may have led to a false self or self-defeating behavior. We can develop new ways to deal with our feelings that can help us find meaningful work, develop intimate relationships, and enjoy a positive sense of self.

Relating These Ideas to Your Own Experience

- What is your earliest memory of feeling ashamed?
- In what ways were your feelings of shame connected to your realization that you were gay or bisexual?
- What was your religious upbringing like? Do you still have any connection to the church you were raised in? What are your current beliefs? If your church was homophobic, how do you

reconcile homophobic religious doctrine with your own spiritual beliefs?
- Can you identify with any of the strategies described in the false-self section? In what ways did they work for you? How have they gotten in your way?
- Have you had experiences in which you felt that you were the object of other gay men's anger or contempt? If you have felt contemptuous of others, are there aspects of yourself that you disdain? Do you associate these with homosexuality?

6

▼

Origins of
Self-Destructive
Behavior

T he obstacles faced by some gay men often have been attributed to our sexual orientation. Problems with substance abuse, low self-esteem, or codependency are not caused by homosexuality, although they may develop as a result of early trauma or homophobic assault.

While it may not have been safe for us to express our feelings as children, emotions continue to press for recognition in adulthood. Unable to reveal themselves directly, they find circuitous pathways to worm into consciousness, often wreaking havoc on the rest of our lives until they are recognized. Self-destructive behavior may be an attempt to ward off repressed feelings of hurt, sadness, and fear. The goal in recovery is to learn how to work through these feelings rather than escape from them.

In this chapter, we will show how the attempt to ward off feelings in response to early abuse can lead to four major types of self-defeating behavior: addiction to alcohol and other substances, compulsive behavior, self-deprivation, and codependency. Each of these may be loosely linked with the false selves described in the previous chapter: Addictions and compulsions may be related to identifying with the aggressor, reactive rebellion, or contempt; self-deprivation can result from withdrawal and isolation; and codependency is a form of overadapting. All of these types of self-destructive behavior are reinforced and driven by the cycle of shame.

The Cycle of Shame

Following is a description of the cycle of shame that can develop as a result of childhood abuse or homophobic assaults, especially if you have never had anyone to talk to about what has happened to you.

1. Internalization of abuse, homophobia, and shame
2. Isolation and the suppression of feelings
3. Development of a false self
4. Warding off feelings through self-destructive behavior
5. Lowered self-esteem and shame

Let's look at how this cycle operates in more detail.

1. *Internalization of abuse, homophobia, and shame*

Unable to counter the onslaught of abuse and homophobia directed at him from his family and peers, a gay youth may internalize these negative messages and feel ashamed.

2. *Isolation and the suppression of feelings*

If a boy could complain about being called a queer and be comforted, he would be able to heal from the assault, instead of feeling ashamed. It is rare for a gay youth to find this level of understanding and comfort in his family, church, or school. Having no adult who could empathize with him, he is likely to suppress his feelings and pretend nothing bothers him.

3. *Development of a false self*

Because he isn't able to express his feelings in a safe environment, he may develop a false self that identifies with the aggressor, rebels, adapts, withdraws, or becomes contemptuous of others in order to cope with a hostile environment.

4. *Warding off feelings through self-destructive behavior*

When the emotions that had been suppressed in response to early abuse begin to emerge, his effort to ward off these feelings can lead to various forms of self-destructive behavior. He may try to escape his sadness, fear, and depression through the use of addictions and compulsions; he may deny that he has any needs through physical and emotional self-deprivation; or he may try to avoid conflict through codependent relationships.

5. *Lowered self-esteem and shame*

Self-destructive behavior produces shame and lowers his self-esteem even further. Already feeling bad about himself, it's all the more difficult to tolerate negative emotions. Unless he gets support to cut through this cycle, he is likely to continue with self-defeating behavior in order to keep these feelings at bay.

To summarize, early abuse and homophobia can lead to the internalization of shame and a poor self-image. Isolation contributes to the suppression of feelings and the development of a false self. Identifying with the aggressor, rebelling, adapting, withdrawing, or feeling contemptuous may have helped you survive your childhood, but eventually your feelings begin to emerge into consciousness. Unless you have adequate support to deal with these emotions, you may try to avoid these feelings through addictions and compulsions, self-deprivation, or codependency. These attempts to escape only compound your sense of shame, which lowers your self-esteem even further. The desire to escape from shameful self-judgment contributes to more self-defeating behavior, and the cycle continues.

Alcohol and Substance Abuse

When memories and emotions emerge from past abuse, some gay men are drawn to chemical substances to avoid the feelings they had in response to early trauma. For someone who was abused as a child or whose emotions were unacceptable to his parents, the use of substances may be an attempt to dissociate from such post-traumatic symptoms as intrusive memories, anxiety, mistrust, and low self-esteem. However, when the drug wears off, the feelings are still there. It takes increasing amounts of the drug to re-create the same effects. The potential for habituation and addiction is very high among survivors of dysfunctional families. Homophobic oppression also contributes to substance abuse. It is estimated that up to one-third of gays abuse alcohol or other substances, which is about three times higher than estimates for the general population.[1]

Not everyone who was abused as a child becomes self-destructive as an adult. Abuse survivors who had supportive adults in their lives may be able to work through the feelings they had in response to the abuse. They don't feel compelled to push their feelings away through the use of alcohol or other substances.

Nor does everyone who develops addictions or compulsions necessarily come from an abusive family. People who feel disconnected from others, have little to look forward to, and who lack meaning in their lives may also be vulnerable to substance abuse. The use of alcohol and other drugs may be stimulated by loss, disappointment, or boredom. Getting high may seem to be a quick fix for emotional conflicts. Even when addictive behavior is not in response to previous problems, addiction tends to take on a life of its own through physiological and psychological dependency. Regardless of the original stimulus, the use of alcohol and drugs can also become self-reinforcing through the cycle of shame.

Some youths get involved with alcohol and drugs to rebel against overly restrictive families or because they feel alienated. Others may identify with alcoholic and drug-abusing parents. Not all experimental drug use by young people leads to alcoholism or other drug abuse. Whether young people will end up abusing chemical substances seems to be related to their level of self-confidence, social skills, and support from their families.[2]

Chemical dependence refers to addiction to drugs or alcohol, but it can also include addiction to substances manufactured within the body, such as adrenalin and dopamine. Some people become addicted to the rush of adrenalin they get from having sex in public, from creating unrealistic deadlines at work, from gambling or stealing, or from other high-risk behavior. Some drugs, such as crack cocaine, act directly on the pleasure center of the brain, depleting the natural supply of dopamine. When his dopamine is depleted, the crack addict becomes depressed, and he finds it even more difficult to experience pleasure from his daily life. He has very little to look forward to and becomes desperate for more drugs.

What many people in recovery discover is that the feelings of pleasure that they sought through drugs are very similar to the feelings of trust, belonging, and love that develop within intimate relationships. They may have learned that relationships weren't very reliable while growing up in a dysfunctional family, but sooner or later they discover that the bottle will also betray them. The alternative is to work through the feelings of hurt from early losses and re-create a life based on the authenticity of the full range of one's emotions. The rush that they depended on from a quick fix is gradually replaced by a deeper satisfaction in work, play, and relationships. Unlike the high from chemical substances, this sense of meaning doesn't disappear when you finish an activity or when you are by yourself.

Compulsive Behavior

Compulsive behavior is the pursuit of any activity to such an extent that it is difficult to control and it interferes with your daily life. Examples include overworking to the point of neglecting relationships and other interests; overeating until you develop health problems; and buying sprees that cause debt to outstrip your income.

Compulsive behaviors can be used to avoid painful emotions. They resemble addictions in the sense that they can be reinforced by the cycle of shame or by the rush of adrenalin mentioned above. They differ from addictions in that you can't simply stop eating, working, or paying bills. It can be difficult to recognize when you are using sex, debt, food, or work to avoid feelings, especially if you're not even aware of the feelings that you are trying to avoid. It helps to look at how the activity fits into the rest of your life and to assess whether or not it seems to be causing disruption. If you think it might be, you can try to stop the behavior or change your pattern and see whether any feelings arise. We will explore ways to get a handle on compulsive behavior in the next chapter.

Sexual Compulsion

In a society that condemns homosexuality, gay men are understandably suspicious of attempts to equate gay sex with sexual compulsion. Gay men have explored a wide range of sexual expression outside of heterosexual models. Some men prefer recreational sex to being in a relationship, meeting their needs for emotional intimacy through friends. Some couples feel it's all right to have sex outside their relationship. Others may enjoy massage or sexual expression with more than one partner. Many gay men are exploring sexuality in a way that is safe, self-aware, and considerate of others.

Some men realize, however, that they are using sex as a drug: they have sex to get high and escape from depression, low self-esteem, or inadequacy, but those feelings are still there when they are finished. Self-loathing may be exacerbated by high-risk sexual behavior through the cycle of shame. A man who uses sex to escape from feelings may be trying to meet his desire for recognition and caring through sex, but he doesn't stick around long enough to become emotionally intimate with anyone. The compulsive substitution of sex for underlying needs is essentially self-defeating.[3]

Possible Sources of Sexual Compulsion

Men who become sexually compulsive may come from very different backgrounds:

- Their families may be sexually repressed, incestuous, or both.
- They may have experienced sexual abuse and ridicule from peers.
- They may not have come from a particularly abusive background, but as adults they learned to sexualize their emotions.

Repressive families. Some families make it clear that sexual thoughts and behavior are sinful and shameful. If a gay youth's parents think that homosexuality is depraved, that masturbation is a mortal sin, and that even sexual feelings are "thought crimes," he has no acceptable sexual outlet. He may conclude that he really is worthless and corrupt, so he decides that he might as well act on his fantasies since he feels ashamed anyway. Driven by shame, he may engage in whatever forms of sexuality his parents would find abhorrent. This is a form of reactive rebellion described in chapter 5.

Sexual abuse. Other families may lack appropriate boundaries, sexualizing their relationships with their children to the point of incest. From early sexual abuse, a young boy may learn that his only value is sexual. Although not everyone who has been sexually abused becomes sexually compulsive, a pattern of compulsive sexuality may emerge in an effort to relive and come to terms with the previous trauma.

An incest survivor may be so conditioned to meeting the sexual desires of others that he's out of touch with his own needs for emotional intimacy. He may have learned that arousal meant that you had sex regardless of the consequences, because that's what was done to him. Since he may have been told how he feels, he lacks confidence in his own perceptions and body signals. He may dissociate during sex, simply going along with whatever someone wants to do with him. If he's not really in touch with his body, he may have a difficult time keeping an erection. His inability to perform may be a signal that he is not really connected to what he is doing.

Shame is reinforced by sexual compulsion. Associating sex with shame, a sexual abuse survivor may seek out sexual contacts in which he is likely to feel degraded. Shame can also stimulate sexual arousal through the fear of getting caught, the excitement of dangerous situations, and the association of sex with humiliation. He may withdraw from sex for a while, but unless he reaches out for support to work through his shame, he continues to use sex to escape from shameful feelings. Sex becomes an all-encompassing obsession, and the cycle continues.

Isolation, low self-esteem, or sexual abuse by peers can also contribute to sexual compulsion. A boy who is identified as a fag or a sissy may be forced by older boys to have sex and be threatened with violence if he tells anyone. When he finally escapes to a big city, he may find a world in which he is no longer put down or humiliated for being a "queer." Instead, he may be admired for his youth and sexual attractiveness. In contrast to his earlier abuse, this flattering attention can be a great relief as well as being very exciting. Lacking the skills he needs to engage men on an emotional level, however, he tries to meet his desire for recognition and affection through his ability to elicit sexual interest. He may be sexually used and then dropped by a succession of men. These rejections may reinforce his belief that sex is all he really has to offer.

Because he doesn't realize that a relationship based on mutual respect is possible, he may continue in this pattern until he recognizes that this strategy isn't working for him. If he can get some support to work through the feelings related to his early abuse, he may be able to improve his social skills and learn how to meet his emotional needs more effectively.

Learning to sexualize emotions. Not all men who become sexually compulsive come from a sexually repressed family or a background of sexual abuse. Men are socialized not to express physical affection, so our desire for affection and longing for physical contact may become sexualized. Sex can be used to express love and affection, but we may confuse our needs for other kinds of attention with having sex. It may be easier to have genital sex than to ask someone to listen to us or to hold us.

It's common for gay men to feel liberated after coming out. A series of sexual adventures doesn't necessarily mean that you're being sexually compulsive. However, the vast opportunity for sexual exploration in big cities has led some men to look to sex as a panacea whenever feelings arise that feel uncomfortable. Instead of talking about how they feel, they learn to sexualize anxiety, conflict, boredom, or depression, but those feelings are still there when they finish having sex. It's easy for gay men who haven't learned how to deal with feelings to become addicted to using sex as a substitute for other emotional needs.

Relapse into Unsafe Sex

Although some men who are sexually compulsive use safer sex, having unsafe sex should cause you to stop and consider why you're having a problem integrating safer sexual practices into your sexual life. This is true for a lot of men, not just for those who are sexually compulsive. A man may relapse into unsafe sex even though he knows all the guidelines. His feelings of panic and remorse may act as a restraint for a while, but unless he gets some help to work through his feelings, he is likely to alternate between abstinence and unsafe sex. He may need a place where he can talk about these difficulties and even grieve the loss of a more spontaneous lifestyle.

It may be difficult to ask for help because he feels ashamed to admit he is having a problem. If he anticipates being judged, he may stay isolated in his shame. Rather than motivating change, the cycle of shame can drive him further into compulsive behavior. The use of alcohol and other drugs to escape from shame can also contribute to poor judgment, denial, and a lack of assertiveness about safer sex. It takes a while to learn how to have healthy and satisfying sex while sober. If he joins a support group where he can talk openly about how he feels, instead of keeping it a secret, he can break the shame cycle and learn how to assert his desire for safer sex.

Some gay couples become lulled into a false sense of security: The lines of what they consider safe begin to blur. They may associate anal sex without a condom with love, commitment, or trust, and forget about the possibility of infection. If they have unsafe sex once or a few times, it becomes harder to maintain their agreed-upon limits. The use of drugs and alcohol can also obscure their determination to stay safe. In some couples, the partner who usually initiates sex may feel insecure. Instead of talking about his feelings, he may be tempted to use unsafe sex as a way to keep his lover interested in him. It may feel awkward to explore his insecurity about his relationship, but trying to hold on to someone by letting him have anal sex without a condom can be life-threatening as well as demeaning. He may need some support to feel confident enough about himself so that he can explore his feelings with his partner and reaffirm his desire for safer sex.

Overwork and Overachieving

The stimulus of keeping busy can also be a way to ward off feelings. When you slow down, feelings begin to emerge, so you get back to work. As a child your sense of self-worth may have been dependent on pleasing your parents. Needing the constant validation engendered by major achievements can arise from a sense of inner emptiness. You may have felt that you had to accomplish something significant to justify your existence. Many people desire meaningful work; but the drive that leads to overachieving may have more to do with appeasement than with self-expression.

When your sense of self is dependent on overachieving, it is vulnerable to the shifting fortunes of success or failure—just as your self-esteem was dependent on how your parents felt about themselves at any particular moment. You can never do or accomplish enough to gain the approval that you never had from your parents. Instead, you can grieve for this loss. This will enable you to balance work that expresses your true interests with rest, recreation, and intimate relationships.

Food, Debt, and Other Compulsions

Food, debt, and other compulsions may arise out of having felt emotionally deprived. The accumulation of possessions is an attempt to make up for that sense of deprivation. You can assuage yourself temporarily with food, travel, and entertainment, but there is no end to the acquisitive nature of compulsive debt, because physical objects cannot make up for being emotionally deprived as a child. You may never be satisfied by buying more, by eating more, or by going on exotic vacations. The feelings left over from early deprivation must be faced and worked through.

Self-Deprivation

Instead of warding off feelings by indulging every impulse, some men go to the opposite extreme. They deprive themselves of food or other basic necessities, wear worn-out clothes, live in dilapidated housing, avoid sex, or stay in dead-end jobs. This is not to say that there is anything wrong with self-sufficiency. Many people try to keep their needs and desires as simple as possible out of political, spiritual, or ecological values. For some men, however, this austere existence can become compulsive in its rigor. They may deprive themselves because they internalized a message of low self-worth, and they don't believe that they deserve anything. Men who felt intruded upon in the past may have learned to avoid sex and intimacy to limit demands by others. Asceticism may be a way to ward off earlier feelings of disappointment and sadness when they learned that they could not depend on anyone.

Even addictive and compulsive overindulgence can be seen as a form of self-deprivation: Although it provides plenty of stimulation, compulsive behavior deprives you of access to your true emotional needs. Escape from feelings may be a reenactment of your parents' inability to tolerate your feelings while you were growing up.

Some people vacillate between overindulgence and severe austerity. They indulge in sex, food, or drugs, and then do penance by denying themselves any comfort. Eventually, they feel so deprived that they burst out again. They have a hard time finding a more moderate existence that allows them some comfort and stimulation, but which doesn't take over their lives. They are not in touch with the underlying feelings that drive the cycle of shame. Instead of working through these feelings, they go from one extreme to the other to avoid them.

Fear of Failure, Fear of Success

Underachieving is common among abuse survivors. It's drummed into their heads that they're no good and will never amount to anything. This can lead to a self-fulfilling prophecy: They don't attempt what they might fail at doing, so they never experience success.

Failure may deflate one's self-esteem, yet success can feel just as threatening. You may get to the point where you've just about achieved your goal, and then sabotage yourself because success might bring on too many demands. Some children in dysfunctional families have to take on adult responsibilities, which leaves them feeling incompetent.

Even if they are perfectly capable of taking on greater challenges as an adult, they may decline a promotion at work because they still feel inadequate.

This sense of childhood inadequacy can lead a survivor of a dysfunctional family to fear being exposed as a fraud. He may believe on a deep level that he was responsible for his family's troubles, and even for his own abuse. It's difficult for him to believe that anyone could genuinely appreciate his accomplishments, because whatever he did as a child was never sufficient. If he has even a modest success, he assumes that it's because he was able to fool everyone. He fears that sooner or later the truth will be discovered: He's an impostor.[4] This fear of being "found out" is common for gays, who often develop a false self to hide their true feelings.

A man may also avoid success out of a sense of survival guilt for transcending his family's dysfunction. He may fear abandonment because he no longer fits into the role prescribed by his family. He was probably emotionally abandoned long ago, and his anxiety over being exposed or abandoned derives from this early loss.[5] Fear of success may have its basis in the unacknowledged grief for not having been appreciated for who he really was.

Western culture reinforces the connection between outward success and self-esteem. Admiration for material success is a poor substitute for an empathic understanding of one's true feelings.[6] A person can easily discount such approval as superficial. It does nothing to counter his assumption that other people wouldn't like him if they really knew him, so he hesitates to reveal himself.

As adults, we may still feel that we have to prove ourselves. Looking outside for approval can be an endless search because outer validation is never enough. The validation we seek from others must eventually come from within. However, receiving support can help us improve our self-esteem if we find people who can empathize with us. An empathic response can help us recognize and accept our feelings. Rather than gauging our self-worth by outward approval, we feel better about ourselves when we can acknowledge how we really feel.

Codependency in Gay Relationships

The concept of codependency developed from an analysis of how partners influence each other in alcoholic relationships. The partner of an alcoholic may attempt to control his lover's drinking, yet be unwilling or unable to set appropriate limits. He colludes with the alcoholic's denial by shielding him from the consequences of his behavior: He covers up for him by calling in to work when he is hungover, he gives him money to buy alcohol, and he makes excuses for him to their friends. No one can control another person's drinking, but no one has to put up with unreliable behavior, either. Hence the label *codependent,* which indicates his part in this system of mutual denial.

Many people who end up in relationships with alcoholics come from alcoholic families themselves. Over time, however, the concept of codependency has been expanded to include anyone's attempt to control another person's behavior, while at the same time being dependent on that person for his own sense of self-worth. This leads to his unwillingness to set limits on what he'll put up with, for fear of abandonment or possible abuse.

Some gay men learn how to survive within a chaotic family or a homophobic culture by discounting their feelings. If you developed an overly adaptive style in response to your parents, you may believe that your own needs aren't really important. A man from a dysfunctional family may be so accustomed to taking care of everyone else's needs that it's hard for him to recognize his own needs or appreciate his own value. There is a lot to be said for considering the needs of others, and if more people did so it would probably be a better world. Codependence, however, is not really about being considerate and helpful: *Codependence is a denial of your own needs in the hope of controlling another person's desire for you.*

Many gay men have found themselves involved with partners who abuse substances or engage in other compulsive behavior. They try to understand and forgive, hoping that their well-meaning influence can provide some stability as well as an incentive for their partner to change. Yet they have a hard time setting limits, and when he doesn't reform, they feel resentful.

Why would someone who was never able to be himself within his own family choose to be a caretaker for a partner who is so unappreciative? As a child, it may have felt too threatening to see his own parents as abusive, so he may be blind to the unreliability of potential partners. A lover who is self-destructive may seem familiar, and he knows how to relate to him. Another possible explanation is that a gay boy who grows up in a dysfunctional family might identify more with his mother and follow her pattern of giving in to her husband rather than standing up to him.

Being attracted to someone who is emotionally unavailable may also be an attempt to restore the loss of a father who withdrew emotionally out of disdain for his gay son. So long as he subjugates his own needs to those of his partner, he has the illusion of holding his interest. He may have some satisfying sexual contact, but his emotional needs are still unmet. Feeling neglected in the present may be an unconscious attempt to resolve and grieve the lack of a nurturing father in the past.

Why would a man who is abusing substances want to be involved with someone who is trying to control him? As a child, he may have identified more with the aggressor (usually the father), or he may be rebelling against being controlled by his family. Finding someone who tries to control his behavior may be an attempt to gain the love and nurturing that he never got from his father. When his partner complains about his behavior, he rebels against any attempt to control him. Yet he may remain in the relationship because he still wants to feel cared for. As much as he rebels against it, he may interpret attempts to control him as emotional interest and caring.

Gay men who develop an adaptive or rebellious stance in response to early abuse may pair up and continue their roles as caretakers and rebels. Each is meeting some of the other's needs, but in a manner that continues to grate on both of them. How can they break through this dynamic to form a mutually caring and nurturing relationship rather than continuing the codependent cycle?

If the caretaker realizes that he is still searching for an unavailable father, for example, he might be able to grieve directly for that loss and be released from further repetition of this pattern in the future. He no longer tries to appease an unavailable partner by discounting his own needs, and he feels good enough about himself to set limits on unreliable behavior. If the rebel can recognize his hurt and rage at being emotionally abandoned, he can grieve for his loss, too, instead of using drugs or rebelling. He doesn't need to have someone trying to control him in order to feel cared for.

Breaking through this pattern is an immense task. It may be difficult for one partner to change unless both partners get support to alter their pattern. In addition to recovery from addictions, compulsions, and codependency, each needs to work through his own family issues. They may also need couples counseling to reach some agreements about mutual expectations in their relationship.

Romantic Addiction

Romantic addiction is being in love with love rather than paying attention to what is actually happening between you and the object of your affection. The relationship addict is often searching for the unconditional love he never received from his parents. If your basic needs for love and acceptance were never met as a child, it's understandable that you would still be searching for a nurturing parent. Unfortunately, we are unlikely to receive unconditional love as an adult. True love can be very accepting, but it has to do with two people meeting each other as equals and getting to know each other as they really are, not as they imagine themselves to be in the "wind-swept heather" of their romantic imaginations.

By grieving for the lack of an understanding parent, you will be less likely to romanticize potential partners. You'll be more likely to find someone you can love as an actual human being, and who appreciates you for who you are.

Repetition Compulsion and Revictimization

When we feel hurt, why would we act in ways that continue the hurt? You would think that we would avoid these patterns rather than repeating them. Repetition, however, gives us opportunities to feel the emotions that we shut away in response to the initial trauma. It is our way of trying to make ourselves understood to precisely those who can't understand us. If you were rejected by your father, for example, you may repeat your abandonment by seeking out men who are not interested in a relationship.

We don't consciously seek out these situations; it's usually only in retrospect that we realize we have repeated a previous pattern. Instead of putting yourself down for getting caught in the same pattern, you can use this recognition to identify the feelings that were left over from the original loss or abuse. By grieving for the current disappointment, you may also work through some of the earlier pain. Healing from trauma won't necessarily stop your attraction to unreliable partners, but you will increase your ability to recognize your pattern earlier. This recognition will help you make a more conscious choice: Do you want to pursue someone who is emotionally unavailable? As you feel better about yourself, you may find that you become increasingly attracted to men who appreciate what you have to offer.

Domestic Violence

Domestic violence has not received a lot of attention in the gay community. Awareness of this problem is slowly beginning to grow because of the development of services for gay batterers and battered partners. As more men speak up about how they have managed to survive and get out of battering relationships, we will see an increased awareness of domestic violence issues in the gay community.

Most models of heterosexual battering include an analysis of male and female socialization that emphasizes the power imbalance between men and women, the sexist assumption of masculine superiority, and a sense of entitlement among men who batter. A relationship between two men may not entail a role-based differential of power, yet many of the dynamics in same-sex domestic violence are similar to those of heterosexual battering: The sense of entitlement, the batterer's displacement of anger onto the battered partner, and the resulting demoralization of the one who is battered are common to abusive relationships of any sexual orientation.

Many batterers come from abusive families themselves. Battering one's partner may be a form of identifying with the aggressor: Instead of working through the feelings of humiliation, anger, and fear from the abuse he experienced as a child, the batterer displaces his anger and frustration onto his partner. The batterer may also be an extreme example of a relationship addict: He concludes that he is worthless when his partner opposes him or threatens to leave him. He may feel as if he will die if he cannot count on the total devotion of his partner.[7] The slightest opposition can send him into a rage. His violence appears to be an attempt to control his lover's behavior, but it is really an act of desperation to ward off devastating feelings of abandonment. His abusive behavior is likely to drive his partner away eventually; thus the batterer re-creates his own worst fear.

Because of the danger of blaming the victim for his own abuse, some survivors and workers in the domestic violence field have challenged the use of the label "codependent" for battered partners.[8] A battered partner doesn't necessarily come from a dysfunctional family.[9] The various coping mechanisms he develops to survive a battering relationship have been described as "battered partner's syndrome" (a form of post-traumatic stress) instead of codependency. It is a misconception to assume that battered partners are psychologically predisposed to find abusive relationships. Symptoms such as minimization of a partner's out-of-control behavior may resemble codependency, but these symptoms often develop as a *result* of being battered.

We can distinguish between codependency, which is the attempt to control *another person's* addictive behavior, and battered partner's syndrome, which is the attempt to control *one's own* behavior to avoid being battered. The battered partner tends to blame himself for the violence. He may have the illusion that if he could only do better, the violence would end. Both partners no doubt contribute to difficulties in their relationship, but conflicts in a relationship do not *cause* domestic violence. *The person who is being battered is not responsible for his partner's violence.* He may hesitate to speak up or end the relationship out of fear that the violence will escalate.[10] He may need legal, social, psychological, and financial support to end the relationship.

Although it's useful to make a distinction between codependency and battered partner's syndrome, it's also true that some codependent people end up in battering relationships. However, neither codependency nor battered partner's syndrome should be used to blame the victim for the violence. The batterer is responsible for his own violence; no one can make another person violent.

Codependency and battered partner's syndrome are learned behaviors in response to dysfunctional and abusive families or partners. They are not an intrinsic part of one's personality.[11] New ideas for protecting oneself from abuse also can be learned. This insight empowers both childhood abuse survivors and abused adults to reach out for support and take control of their own lives instead of feeling permanently victimized by their abuse.

Many batterers abuse alcohol and other substances. The use of alcohol may lessen the inhibitions of a batterer so that he is more likely to strike out in anger, but alcohol and drugs do not cause violence. Batterers must stop using alcohol and drugs if they want to stop their violent behavior, but they must also learn other ways to deal with their anger.[12] Some battered partners abuse alcohol and other substances as a way to cope with domestic violence. They also need to get into recovery to assess clearly what their options are for keeping themselves safe.

Relating These Ideas to Your Own Experience

- Do you see ways in which your behavior patterns resemble the cycle of shame? How do they differ?
- Can you identify times when you used alcohol, drugs, sex, or food to escape from feelings?
- In what ways do you think you may be depriving yourself or holding yourself back from your true interests?
- Do you find that you consistently deny your own needs in deference to those of others?
- What are your expectations about what a relationship can provide for you?
- Have you been in relationships where you repeated previously unproductive patterns? What were the underlying desires you

hoped to meet? Can you identify issues in your family that these patterns remind you of?

- Have you ever been ridiculed, threatened, or touched in ways that you didn't like by your partner? If you feel too threatened to object, you may need some help to keep yourself safe. See appendix II for referrals.

Part II

Reclaiming
Your Life

7

▼

Understanding the Process of Healing

We have looked at various ways in which gay men may have been traumatized while growing up in dysfunctional families within a homophobic culture. With no one to talk to who could help them make sense of their abuse, some gay men get caught in a cycle of shame and self-destructive behavior. Understanding the nature of post-traumatic stress can provide some insight about how you managed to survive. This insight can motivate recovery by helping you realize that you are not simply a victim of the past. Healing from previous trauma will provide you with choices about how you want to live your life as an adult. Some people understand why they developed certain problems, but they have a hard time putting this awareness into practice. Insight is useful, but it is generally not sufficient to sustain recovery. It's helpful to have an overview of the healing process, so you don't experience doubts, discouragement, or an occasional slip as a reason to give up. What follows is an outline of the aspects of healing you are likely to encounter in the process of recovery from dysfunctional and homophobic families.

Stages of Healing

1. Acknowledge abuse
2. Identify post-traumatic effects
3. Recognize self-destructive behavior
4. Get support for recovery
5. Work through feelings
6. Counter shame and negative messages
7. Combat homophobia and heterosexism
8. Learn how to nurture yourself
9. Assert your own needs
10. Create your own life

1. Acknowledge abuse. Acknowledging abuse involves making a personal assessment of the ways in which you may have been abused by your family or suffered from homophobic assaults. It can also be a recognition of how you wish you could have been cared for and treated as a gay youth who was first becoming aware of same-sex attractions. While you were reading chapters 1 through 3, which provide a guide for identifying various types of abuse, you may have discovered some insights into your personal experiences.

2. Identify post-traumatic effects. If you were abused as a child, you may suffer from some post-traumatic symptoms that stem from early abuse. Look through the list of symptoms in chapter 4 and consider ways in which you may have been affected by abuse, neglect, and homophobia. You might also want to look through the effects listed in Appendix II.

3. Recognize self-destructive behavior. Be open with yourself about whether you use substances or certain behaviors to push away feelings.

Consider whether you are really in control, or whether you are rationalizing and denying the role of drugs and sex in suppressing your emotional life. Also, look at tendencies toward taking care of others at the expense of your own needs and see whether you might be depriving yourself. Consider whether you may have identified with the aggressor in your treatment of others. Chapters 5 and 6 may have helped you see the link between the cycle of shame and self-destructive behavior.

4. Get support for recovery. It's important to end your isolation. When you have people in your life who understand and support your recovery, you'll feel safer getting in touch with feelings. As you feel more confident revealing yourself as you really are, you won't feel the need to present a false self to the world. In chapter 8, you'll read about the importance of support in recovery from addictions and compulsions. Chapter 11 provides an overview of what to expect in individual and group psychotherapy.

5. Work through feelings. When you stop self-destructive behavior, you gain more access to your emotional life. This allows healing to take place, so you no longer feel compelled to escape from yourself. You become more authentic as you allow yourself to feel your emotions rather than letting them control you. Getting in touch with your emotional response to early trauma and developing access to your feelings will be the focus of chapter 9.

6. Counter shame and negative messages. When you stop using substances or compulsions to push away feelings, you may get in touch with negative and homophobic messages. In chapter 10 you will develop your ability to recognize when you are putting yourself down, to understand the protective function of critical voices, and to develop strategies for challenging the negative messages that you may have internalized as a child.

7. Combat homophobia and heterosexism. For gay men, it is important to recognize the influence of both external and internalized homophobia on our self-esteem and emotional development. Instead of taking your anger and rage out on others or on yourself, you can learn how to use your anger more effectively to challenge institutional discrimination. Chapter 9 offers some practical ideas for dealing with anger and chapter 12 looks at how we can combat homophobia in the wider society.

8. Learn how to nurture yourself. If you never had your basic needs met for dependable nurturing, love, empathy, and acceptance, you can still become your own nurturing parent. You can also take care of yourself in many practical ways: by eating well, getting enough rest, getting exercise, and finding enjoyable forms of recreation. Chapter 10 will help you accept and appreciate your own child self through self-affirming thoughts, goals, and behaviors.

9. Assert your own needs. You can learn how to recognize your own boundaries and set appropriate limits in current relationships, as well as with those who have abused you in the past. In chapter 12 you will gain a sense of your own personal rights so that you can end the cycle of revictimization and reach out for help if you get caught in abusive interactions.

10. Create your own life. It takes a lot of effort to deal with issues from the past, but it takes even more energy to avoid the effects of early abuse through self-defeating behavior. As you heal from early abuse and internalized homophobia, you gradually feel released to discover your true interests. The last section of chapter 12 looks at some of the ways you can begin to create your own life.

These tasks don't necessarily follow in order. For example, some people remember early abuse after they stop using alcohol or other drugs to blot out their memories. Some people don't stop using alcohol until they reach out for support. You may also find that you come back to previous issues and reexperience them more deeply once you have made progress in other areas. As you get more in touch with feelings, you may gain more access to earlier memories. Identifying post-traumatic effects may help you counter self-blame. When you uncover self-defeating patterns, you may discover other ways to take care of your true emotional needs.

These skills build on one another—as you recognize the effects of previous abuse, you may become more determined to assert your needs in your current relationships. When you counter internalized homophobia, you may open up a vast network of support from other gay men. As you reach out for support, it becomes easier to work through your feelings, counter negative messages, and nurture yourself.

There will no doubt also be times when you feel discouraged about your progress. This is a natural part of healing. You can use your doubts to get in touch with the source of your frustration. It also helps to receive some acknowledgment for how difficult this process can be at times. When you are focused on how much there is still to do, you may forget or not really appreciate how much work you have already accomplished. Reaching out to others can help you gain some perspective on the progress you have already made, and provide you with more confidence as you continue the process of reclaiming your life.

8

▼

Recovery from Addictions
and Compulsions

If you were abused as a child, you did the best you could to survive a dysfunctional family or homophobic assault. You may have shut off your feelings in response to this trauma, but these emotions do not really disappear. As you grow older, your feelings begin to work their way into consciousness. You feel bad, not really knowing why, and you may push these feelings away through the use of drugs or compulsive behavior. As an adult, you can heal from childhood trauma by working through the feelings that were too dangerous to feel while you were being abused. To gain access to these feelings, however, you need to stop pushing them away through the use of substances or compulsive behavior. In this chapter, we will look at how to get the support you need to recover from addictions and compulsions.

Reluctance to Seek Help

Support is an essential aspect of recovery. You gain access to a community of people who are making changes in their lives rather than simply reacting to the past. Their experience, acceptance, and understanding can help you handle the feelings that emerge when you stop using drugs or compulsive behavior to push them away. It may be difficult, however, for some men to recognize their need for help. Male socialization, mixed messages about drugs, and homophobia can reinforce denial and contribute to your reluctance to reach out for support.

Male Socialization

Self-sufficiency is strongly ingrained in male socialization. Men are expected to be stoic in the face of loss, disappointment, or fear. Any admission of pain or vulnerability is associated with dependency. Men may not admit even to themselves that they feel sad or hurt, and they are reluctant to disclose self-doubt to anyone. Gay men in particular learn very early that it is dangerous to reveal their true feelings to other males.

We may take pride in independent achievement, but sometimes independence can be isolating and self-defeating. Only one-third of psychotherapy clients are men. Women more frequently try to commit suicide, but more men actually kill themselves because they won't reach out for help. For many men, refusing to get help for addictions can become a form of gradual suicide.

Mixed Messages about Drugs

In the United States, we get a lot of mixed messages about substance abuse. Alcohol is licensed, but marijuana is illegal. The government subsidizes tobacco farmers, but sends in troops to confiscate marijuana plants. Tobacco and alcohol are each responsible for death tolls many times the combined death rates attributed to the use of other drugs.[1] People are encouraged to use tranquilizers and pain medications for symptoms that often can be alleviated by recognizing feelings, stress-reduction, and learning how to relax.

The war on drugs is oriented toward eliminating the supply of illegal substances and tends to ignore the underlying social and psychological forces that contribute to substance abuse. Young people are encouraged to "just say no," while at the same time they are provided with few resources to help them recognize and handle their emotions more constructively. Ethnic minorities need greater opportunities for meaningful work to engage their talents and interests. Gay youths need to have their sexual orientation recognized and supported so that they don't feel compelled to escape from their feelings.

Sex-Negative and Homophobic Attitudes

Sex roles evolve within a culture to regulate social functioning. Yet many of these sexual rules are oppressive to gay men, so we break them and risk becoming outcasts. Since we already function outside the usual social norms, why not explore the outer limits of what is possible in gay relationships? Throughout the sexual revolution of the 1970s, many gay men questioned traditional roles by trying out alternative lifestyles. Being openly gay is itself a challenge to the usual boundaries that exist between men in our culture. Massage, sexual friendships, bisexuality, and committed gay relationships (both sexual and nonsexual) are among the various ways to express intimacy. Who knows what might be possible in relationships between gay men?

The trouble is that some men have gotten lost while exploring this uncharted sexual territory. Recovery from sexual compulsion is not about subscribing to heterosexual norms or denying your sexuality. Recovery can become a healing journey that will help you discover and express your true sexual and emotional needs.

Denial

If it was dangerous to express yourself as a child, you may have started to use drugs to ward off feelings with little awareness that you were doing so. Because of the mixed messages about the use of drugs in our culture, it may be difficult to recognize when your use of substances or other behavior is a problem. For some men, it's easier to apologize for what they did while they were drunk than it is to admit that their use of alcohol is out of control. They say they are sorry, but continue to drink. Denial also is reinforced by the mind-altering effects of the drug itself. Alcohol and drug addiction can lead to lapses in memory, euphoric recall of drunken behavior, repression of feelings, and poor judgment.

Despite the contradictions in our society about drug use and sexuality, many gay men have realized that their use of substances or sexual activity has taken on a compulsive character, and they are willing to reach out for support. Recovery meetings specifically for gays are available in larger cities, and even mixed meetings are usually nonjudgmental and open to gay participation. There are also gay-sensitive and sex-positive support groups for sexual compulsion.

The Strategic Use of Will

Willpower is rarely sufficient to stop addictions. Alcohol and other substances not only push away your feelings but also impair your judgment. When you've already had a drink, it's no longer "you" who is deciding whether to have another. This doesn't mean that your will is totally useless, however. You can learn how to use your willpower by deciding to get support *before* you have a drink rather than trying to control how much you drink after you begin. In early recovery, it's useful to stay in clean and sober settings to avoid being tempted to drink or use by peer pressure or by all the familiar cues associated with a using lifestyle, which can be extremely difficult to resist. You can identify and avoid the kinds of situations that are likely to tempt you into compulsive behavior.

Coming to terms with addictions and compulsions is not just a matter of avoiding temptation, however. You may be sitting at home and still feel an incredible desire to have sex, binge, or escape from your feelings by getting drunk. Recovery involves gaining access to your emotional life so that you're not as tempted to escape from your feelings in the first place. Get the support you need to tolerate the emergence of underlying feelings by using your will to:

- Reach out for support and develop a clean and sober social network
- Identify "bottom-line" compulsive behavior and stay away from tempting situations
- Expand the moment between impulse and action so that you have more conscious control over your behavior

Let's explore these points.

Support for Recovery

It can be extremely difficult to stop addictions or compulsive behavior by yourself. You may stop for a while but then lose sight of why you are struggling so hard, especially when feelings arise that you had previously managed to keep at bay. It's very easy to fall back into denial about whether your substance use or behavior is really a problem without consistent support for working through underlying feelings. Chemically dependent people often get to the point where their lives are completely unmanageable before they are able to realize that their addictive behavior is destroying them.

Gay men enter recovery at various points. Some hit bottom through the intervention of the court, a medical crisis, the loss of a relationship, or some other dramatic experience that forces them to reevaluate their priorities.[2] As awareness about recovery resources has increased in the gay community, some men are able to recognize at an earlier stage that their use of substances is self-destructive. They may learn from their friends or in psychotherapy that they are using substances or compulsive behavior to push feelings away, and this realization allows them to reach out for support.

Getting in touch with feelings is part of the natural healing process, but it can be frightening. It may not have been safe for you as a child to express or even feel your emotions. You may have started to use alcohol or other drugs as a way to avoid painful feelings. It may be difficult to tolerate the feelings that begin to arise when you stop using. That's no reason to give up—but it's a very good reason to reach out to others for support. Getting support will help you work through these feelings rather than using drugs or compulsive behavior to avoid them.

Some men hesitate to reach out for support because they see themselves as being different from others, or they anticipate shame and rejection. They wonder if they are the only ones who ever felt certain emotions or made such awful mistakes. Other men in recovery have had similar experiences with their addictions or compulsions, so you can say how you feel without fear of being judged. A recovery group can help you see that your life and your insights are important. Revealing one's innermost doubts, fears, and conflicts helps release others from their intense emotional isolation. Rather than being judged, most men in recovery groups feel appreciated for being authentic with their emotions. Despite the rejection you may have experienced from your own family, you find meaning in your new relationships. You realize that you matter to other people, and that other people matter to you. As you build trust in the group, you may find that you are more able to accept and give support outside of the meetings as well.

Recovery Resources

Alcoholics and Narcotics Anonymous, Save Our Sobriety, and professionally run treatment centers all provide a community of support that breaks your isolation. In most communities, you can find meetings to attend every day of the week, as well as arrange to call someone whenever you are tempted to use.

Alcoholics and Narcotics Anonymous

Alcoholics Anonymous (AA) is the oldest and most accessible recovery program. It is free and confidential, with meetings readily available all over the world. These groups have no professionally trained facilitator, but they have a clear twelve-step format that provides some structure and keeps the meeting in focus.[3] Group members take turns talking about how they have dealt with the feelings and problems they are faced with. No one, however, is required to talk. You can sit and listen until you feel comfortable enough to participate. Most groups discourage "cross-talk," or discussion between members, in the belief that simply having the chance to speak and be heard is healing in itself.

In addition to meetings, you can also get individual support through AA's sponsorship program. You can ask someone who has been in the group for a while to be your sponsor, so you have someone to talk to when feelings come up and you are tempted to use. Don't be shy to reach out for help; it's not an imposition. Sponsorship is considered an important part of the program. Helping others through rough times reinforces the sponsor's own recovery.

Save Our Sobriety

Save Our Sobriety, or SOS (also known as Secular Organizations for Sobriety) is a more recently developed self-help group that believes recovery can be treated as an issue separate from the spiritual concerns addressed by AA and other twelve-step programs (see the section below on The Higher Power and the Nurturing Self). SOS believes that recovery is possible by recognizing that you have a drinking problem, accepting it, and making sobriety your number-one priority. Making sobriety your first priority means that despite how you feel in response to disappointments, arguments, or loss, you don't drink or use "no matter what."[4] Instead, you reach out for support.

Inpatient and Outpatient Programs

For people who have serious detoxification problems or who have not been able to make effective use of self-help groups, inpatient programs are available that can break the cycle of addiction. They usually last one to six months and provide support similar to that of AA within a residential setting. Inpatient programs have professional addiction care providers and are covered by some medical insurance. Aftercare programs help you maintain your sobriety as you make the transition to your own support groups in the community. In many large cities, gay recovery professionals have developed outpatient alcohol and substance abuse clinics specifically for gay men. They offer therapy groups in addition to regular support meetings. These groups can help you deal with underlying feelings as well as provide a clean and sober setting for socializing.

Resources for Recovery from Compulsive Behavior

Other twelve-step groups that address compulsive behavior include Overeaters Anonymous, Debtors Anonymous, and Sex and Love Addicts Anonymous. SOS welcomes people who wish to work on compulsive behaviors of any type, not just alcohol or drug addiction, and is gradually forming more specialized groups. Some professionally led therapy groups are also available for gay men who are sexually compulsive.

Phases in Recovery

Recovery takes place in two main phases.[5] The first phase is getting support to stop the addictive or compulsive behavior. The second phase is beginning to work through the feelings that arise when you stop using substances or compulsive behavior to push feelings away.

Early Recovery

During most of the first year of recovery, your main focus is on staying sober. You need to establish a support system to stop your addiction. Support may include self-help as well as group therapy focused on recovery. You can go to meetings every day, or even twice a day if that's what it takes to stay sober. As your body cleanses itself, you may experience withdrawal symptoms such as restlessness, sleeplessness, and tremors. Withdrawal from some drugs, such as alcohol and Valium, may require medical supervision.

Some men experience a rocky entry into their emotional life. A man in early recovery may become argumentative at work, get into physical fights, get thrown out of his apartment, have accidents, and generally create chaos in his life to ward off the feelings that begin to emerge when he stops using. A "dry drunk" refers to someone who has stopped drinking but who continues with compulsions or other addictions to escape from his feelings. Some of these may include smoking, debt, gambling, or excessive use of coffee, sugar, sex, or food. You need support to work through feelings rather than substituting one addiction for another. It's also important to eat balanced meals, get plenty of exercise, and lots of rest.

Second Phase Recovery

The next phase of recovery involves dealing with the issues that contributed to your problems in the first place. When you stop drinking, you may be flooded with feelings that you are not accustomed to dealing with. With the support of your group and sponsor, you learn how to identify and communicate your emotions, instead of just acting on them or escaping them by taking drugs.

Many people's normal adolescent development stopped when they started drinking. Recovery is a lot like being a teenager again. You need to reexperience and complete the tasks of adolescence in sobriety. Even if you are already physically separated from your parents, you begin to form your own identity apart from them, instead of just reacting against them. You develop a network of friends and come to terms with your sexual orientation.[6] As you gain more practice in identifying feelings, you will increase your ability to ask for what you want and negotiate agreements in intimate relationships.

Gaining Control over Compulsive Behavior

Recovery from compulsive behavior and early abuse depends on free access to your emotions. You will need to get a handle on drug and alcohol addictions before you will be able to recover from other compulsive behavior; otherwise you won't be able to tolerate the feelings that arise when you stop using work, food, debt, or sex to escape from your feelings. Sobriety should be your first priority.

Compulsive behavior and substance abuse both push away feelings, and some behaviors can take on an addictive quality similar to chemical addictions. However, behavioral compulsions differ from substance abuse in that they have fewer mind-altering effects. Moreover, they are often activities that we can't simply abstain from. No one ever needs to take another drink of alcohol, for example; but we all need to eat, most of us need to work, and sex is a healthy part of intimate relationships. It's not always easy to tell when you are being compulsive about these behaviors.

It helps to come up with your own guidelines for "bottom-line behaviors" that will indicate to you when you are acting compulsively. The following section will help you identify the point at which you are likely to engage in various kinds of compulsive behavior. Then we will look at some techniques that will increase your ability to recognize your impulses instead of automatically acting on them. You will learn how to identify the underlying feelings so that you can make a *conscious choice* about your behavior.

Identifying Bottom-Line Behaviors

A "bottom-line behavior" is an indication that your behavior is becoming compulsive. Bottom-line behaviors are unique to each individual. You may want to get ideas and solicit feedback from others, but only you can identify the point at which your behavior is out of control.

Food. If eating has been a problem, Overeaters Anonymous can help you identify how you use food to escape from feelings. Do you snack continually on junk food? Do you alternate between starving yourself with crash diets and bingeing? Do you eat whatever is in front of you without thinking about it? Make a list of behaviors that will indicate to you that you are at risk for eating compulsively (remember that those listed below are just examples—you need to come up with your own list):

- Buying a gallon of ice cream and eating most of it in one sitting
- Eating mindlessly while watching hours of TV
- Going to the kitchen after an argument
- Bingeing and purging

After identifying your bottom-line behaviors, you can create a plan for noncompulsive eating. For example, you might keep wholesome food in the house, shop when you're *not* hungry, and eat at regular times. You might want to eat without reading, watching TV, or other distractions. Instead of going to the kitchen when you have an argument, go to your bedroom and write down your feelings, or call your sponsor.

Some people confuse a desire for nurturing with hunger. You might want to put a sign on the refrigerator that says *"What is it, besides food, that you are really hungry for right now?"* These agreements with yourself will help you gauge when you are using food to nurture yourself or to stuff down feelings, instead of eating because you are naturally hungry. You can get a sponsor to help you with your plan and arrange to have people to call when you are tempted to violate your agreements. You can talk about the feelings that are emerging instead of avoiding them by eating. You can find healthier ways to nurture yourself. If you end up bingeing anyway, you can stop the shame cycle by recognizing your feelings instead of putting yourself down.

Debt. If compulsive debt is your problem, with the help of Debtors Anonymous you can identify ways in which you use credit compulsively. Do you buy from mail-order catalogues? Do you spend your lunch hour shopping? Do you buy on impulse? When you figure out ways in which you use debt inappropriately, you can come up with specific agreements with yourself for handling purchases. For example, you might want to cancel all but one major credit card, stop getting mail-order catalogues, limit your credit card use to certain types of purchases, stop buying on impulse, and leave your credit card at home when you go shopping. If you find that you are about to violate one of these agreements, call your sponsor instead to talk about how you are feeling. Do you feel deprived? What are some other ways that you could nurture yourself so that you feel emotionally taken care of?

Sex. It can be difficult to gauge when you are being sexually compulsive. Male socialization tends to separate sexuality from emotional bonding, so you may not be sure how you really feel. How do you distinguish a normal sex drive from sexual compulsion?

You can start by assessing ways in which you think your sexuality is obviously out of control. Do you masturbate many times throughout the day? Do you feel compelled to use pornography? Do you put yourself in dangerous situations or engage in illegal activity? Do you have frequent anonymous sex that leaves you feeling ashamed or unsatisfied? Do you have trouble insisting on safer forms of sex? Do you violate your own standards about appropriate times and places for sexual activity? Do you have sex in the bushes or in bathrooms when what you really want is to be listened to or held?

In early recovery from sexual compulsion, some men find it helpful not to have sex at all for a while just to let themselves cool off. Then they set up some guidelines to help them identify times when they are likely to use sex compulsively. For example, if you are tempted to masturbate in the steam room at the gym, you could decide to change your clothes and shower at home. You could avoid walking through certain parks or using restrooms where you are likely to have anonymous sex. If pornography has been an obsession, you may want to cancel your magazine subscriptions and get rid of your videos. You might want to go to a safer sex workshop to learn how to ask for what you want and negotiate safer sex. You can go to support groups such as Sex and Love Addicts Anonymous to learn how to identify your underlying emotions instead of acting on them. If you find yourself in a tempting situation, you may find that talking about your feelings interrupts the ritual of anonymous sex. Over time, you will learn to recognize when your desire for sex is being driven by the cycle of shame and when it is a natural response to sexual interest in another man.

Romance. It can be difficult to tell whether you are using romance in a compulsive manner. Everyone loves being in love. While ''chemistry'' can be an important ingredient in romance, for some people an immediate surge of attraction may be a sign that you should slow down a bit to let your emotions catch up with your hormones. If you tend to fall in and out of stormy relationships, you might want to create some strategies for getting to know someone first before you become sexually and romantically involved. For example, you could decide to date a man a few times before you have sex with him. This is not always easy in gay relationships, since some men expect to have sex right away or not at all. You may need to talk about your pattern and how you're trying to do things differently.

New relationships can be exciting, but they can also produce anxiety. You may feel self-conscious with a man you find attractive. It may seem easier to have sex than to talk about how you feel. However, you can learn how to be aware of your attraction without having sex immediately. Intimacy is based not only on sexual attraction but also on your ability to listen to each other, disclose feelings, and negotiate agreements. You can allow yourself the gradual progression of getting to know someone first as an acquaintance, then as a friend, and eventually as a romantic partner.

Some early recovery programs include group socializing such as picnics, dances, and sports. These events help you get to know a variety of men in nonthreatening contexts. The expectation is that you will not become sexually involved with the men in your support group. You get some practice being in touch with friendly and affectionate feelings toward other men without acting on them sexually. At the same time, you learn how to take care of some of your needs for emotional intimacy. When you are ready for a sexual and romantic relationship, you will have had some experience in dealing with the feelings that are likely to arise when you become intimately involved with another man.

Be alert to the signals that you are putting yourself at risk for acting out: After an argument or other disappointment, you get a carton of ice cream out of the freezer; you take your credit card with you to go shopping; you bring work home from the office; you go into the steam room at the gym after working out. There's nothing wrong with any of these actions in and of themselves; you need to identify your own bottom-line behaviors. You can use a transgression of your agreements as a signal to realize that you must be having feelings that you are trying to push away and that it's time to reach out for support. You put away the ice cream, the credit card, the extra work; you take a whirlpool instead of the steam bath; then you call your sponsor or go to a meeting.

Making a connection between the impulse to act compulsively and the underlying feeling is an important element in gaining more control over compulsive behavior. Recognizing the impulse to act *before* you act is not always easy to do. It takes some practice to develop your ability to identify the impulse before you act. Let's look at some ideas for increasing your ability to recognize this moment.

Expanding the Moment Between Impulse and Action

As mentioned earlier, simply avoiding temptation may not be enough to alter an ingrained pattern. You may stay away from parks and restrooms, but then see someone who interests you just walking down the street. Before you've even had time to think about whether it's a good idea, you make eye contact, go back to your apartment, and have sex. For some people, compulsive behavior occurs in a trancelike state that blocks consideration of reasonable alternatives.[7] As in the examples below, impulse slides into action without any intervening thought or awareness:

- You feel like having a drink, and you do so without questioning it.
- You have an impulse to eat, so you eat without even thinking about it.
- You see something you want and you buy it even if you can't afford it.
- You become aroused by a man and you have sex whether or not it's an appropriate time or place, regardless of how you really feel toward him.

To get in touch with your feelings instead of acting on your impulses, you need to be able to recognize the impulses. Listening to other people's stories in recovery groups is one way to expand your ability to recognize your impulses. Thinking about your own behavior after the fact is another. Instead of getting down on yourself when you slip up, try to identify the feelings that led to the impulse. What follows is a five-step plan for developing this observing part of yourself, which can help you expand the moment between impulse and action:

1. Impulse
2. Recognize that you are having an impulse
3. Get in touch with underlying feelings
4. Decide whether to act on the impulse
5. Reach out for support

1. Impulse. At first, you simply have an impulse:

- I "need" a drink.
- Let's eat.
- I want that.
- Let's have sex.

2. Recognize that you are having an impulse. Instead of immediately acting on it, recognize that you are having an impulse:

- I'm aware that I want a drink.
- I'm aware that I'd like to eat.
- I'm aware that I'd like to buy that.
- I'm aware that I'm sexually aroused.

3. Get in touch with underlying feelings. The next step is to identify underlying feelings that may have motivated the impulse:

- My date stood me up. I feel hurt, and I want to bolster my self-esteem.
- I feel disappointed because I didn't get the raise I expected, and I was going to stuff myself to feel satisfied by something.
- I feel deprived because I've been working so hard on all this recovery, and I want to treat myself.
- I feel lonely, and I want some comforting.

4. Decide whether to act on the impulse. By becoming aware of the feelings that led to the desire, you can decide whether you want to act on your impulse:

- Having a drink may pick me up for a moment, but I'm only going to feel worse about myself later. I'll call my sponsor instead.
- It's true that I'm disappointed, but I am really hungry. I'll put the ice cream away and have a decent meal.
- No, I can't afford to buy anything, but maybe there's another way I could treat myself. I'll go for a walk along the river at sunset.
- That guy is hot, but I don't even know him. If what I really want is some comfort, I'm not likely to get it from a stranger. I could call a friend instead.

5. Reach out for support. Then you reach out for support. You call your sponsor or a friend, or go to a meeting and talk about the feelings that led to your impulse. Reaching out for support helps you *end your isolation*. You *interrupt the shame cycle* by not acting on your impulse, and you *take care of yourself* by addressing your underlying needs. You deserve recognition for making progress on changing some very difficult patterns.

If you acted on your impulse, talk about it in your support group so that you can identify the underlying feelings. You don't need to berate yourself for not being perfect. Recognizing the slip is progress in itself. Talking about it instead of keeping it a secret will help alleviate your sense of shame, and you'll feel less of a need to escape from your feelings into more self-destructive behavior. Hindsight can help you use the slip to expand the moment between impulse and action in the future. You may also become aware of a link between previous trauma and your current feelings. You can make a conscious decision about what you would like to do in response to your emotions and impulses.

You don't need to wait until you spontaneously have an impulse to practice expanding the moment between impulse and action. It's easier to incorporate new behavior into the rest of your life when you practice skills during a moment *when you are not overwhelmed* by your desire: You've already eaten, for example, or you've recently had sex. You imagine having a desire, then go through the steps outlined above. (You may feel less tempted to act on your desire if you describe these steps to your therapist or sponsor, especially when you are first starting out.) It also helps to write down your responses to these suggestions.

Developing your ability to expand the moment between impulse and action increases your capacity for delayed gratification. It also helps you address your true underlying feelings and needs. Instead of an instant jolt of drugs or an adrenalin rush, you begin to appreciate more subtle forms of sensuous stimulation: When you eat in response to natural hunger rather than stuffing yourself, you really taste your food. Instead of blindly going through the day, you notice the sights, smells, and sounds of your surroundings. Rather than having sex just to get off, you become aware of your emotional and sensual connection to another man.

The Higher Power and
the Nurturing Self

Alcoholics Anonymous and Save Our Sobriety represent two different philosophies in approaching recovery. AA offers a twelve-step program that encourages members to recognize that they are powerless to control their drinking. Members turn their lives over to a "higher power" that will help them remain sober since they have not been able to accomplish this on their own.[8] Seeing the source of power outside of themselves has helped many people give up trying to control their addictions. They realize that their own efforts to moderate their use have gotten them nowhere, and it's a relief to admit that they can't control their use of alcohol or drugs.

AA members often say, "take what you like, and leave the rest." Members of AA and other twelve-step programs are encouraged to think of God or their higher power in whatever way they find meaningful. If you don't believe in God, the "power greater than ourselves" can be understood as the fellowship of other people in recovery who are available when you feel overwhelmed or tempted to use.

Some people find the concept of a higher power difficult to accept even with this disclaimer. In recovery from early abuse, homophobia, and addictions, they wish to empower themselves. This has led to the development of agnostic twelve-step meetings and groups such as SOS that do not refer to a higher power. SOS contends that recovery from addiction should be a separate issue from religion or spirituality.

AA emphasizes faith in a higher power that can help you once you admit that you are powerless to control your addictions. SOS emphasizes taking personal responsibility for making sobriety a daily priority. Despite the difference in approach, both AA and SOS offer hope and group support in the process of recovery.

Both approaches can be understood as ways to develop your own self-awareness. Whether you believe that it is a wise and nurturing part of yourself or it is God who helps you recognize your impulse, this recognition increases your ability to identify your underlying feelings and make conscious choices about your behavior.

We have a natural capacity to heal once we stop using substances or compulsive behavior to push our feelings away. However, coping with the emotions that arise when you stop using is not easy to do on your own. If you learned to escape from your emotions by using substances, food, or sex, you are likely to start using again despite your best intentions unless you reach out for support. By tapping into the vast resource of other people in recovery, you empower yourself in your own process of healing.

Spirituality and the Search for Meaning

Finding meaning in your life can provide a powerful motivation for healing from abuse and addictions. Spiritual traditions have historically provided a sense of meaning and cohesiveness in a society, yet many gays feel alienated from homophobic religions. However, spirituality doesn't require specific religious beliefs. You may find personal meaning in compassion, love, trust, appreciation of nature, your own relationship with God, or faith in the human spirit. These values can instill a sense of purpose over the long journey toward reclaiming your true nature, which may have been damaged by early trauma and obscured by addictions or compulsive behavior.

During the initial phase of sobriety, it may be difficult to identify any sense of purpose in your life except to stay sober. When you are no longer using addictions or compulsions to push feelings away, you are confronted by raw emotion without your usual escapes or defenses. Initial feelings of boredom, restlessness, and anxiety may give way to anger, sadness, and hurt. In the midst of this emotional turmoil, it may be difficult to understand what other people are referring to when they talk about healing. Not knowing what else there is to look forward to, life can seem meaningless. This state of inner emptiness can be compared with the "dark night of the soul" referred to in some religious traditions.[9] It can also be thought of as an existential crisis, or a crisis in personal meaning.

If you never felt understood or appreciated in the past, it really is a leap of faith to reach out for support. Whether that faith is in God, the fellowship of others, or simply in your own capacity to heal, it is possible to move through this anguish and come out on the other side when you get support to stay sober one day at a time. You gradually learn that you can survive feelings without using drugs or compulsive behavior to push them away. You begin to discover your own source of meaning by exploring your true interests and becoming involved with other people.

Relating These Ideas to Your Own Experience

- How do you feel about reaching out for support from others? What are some of your hesitations? What kind of contact with other people feels supportive to you?
- Who in your life right now can you call when you are tempted to use?
- In this chapter, we talked about various ways to recognize when you are being compulsive with certain behaviors. Can you identify clues that would suggest to you that you may be using sex, work, food, or debt compulsively?

- See if you can recognize an impulse, identify underlying feelings, and decide how you want to respond.
- What are your own beliefs about a higher power, or about your own nurturing self?
- What is the role of spirituality or a sense of meaning in your own recovery?

The attempt to control drinking or compulsions often fails because you are trying to control your feelings through the addiction. Realizing that you don't need to control how you feel can be a great relief. In the next chapter, we will explore ways to cope with the emotions that are likely to emerge when you stop pushing your feelings away.

9
▼

Working Through
Feelings

Much of the work in recovery from dysfunctional and homophobic families involves coming to terms with feelings that you may have repressed because it wasn't safe to expose your true self while you were growing up. When feelings are no longer pressing for acknowledgment, you're less likely to act in a self-defeating manner. This gives you the freedom to grow and create your own life rather than reacting against the past. In this chapter, we will look at how to work with your emotions so that you can come to terms with the feelings you had in response to the original trauma and heal from early abuse.

Why Deal with Any of This?

Some men figure that nothing can be done to change what's already happened, so why dwell on the past? The point in recovery from childhood trauma is not to change the past, but to work through feelings *that continue to influence your life today.* When you stop warding off feelings through addictions and compulsions, memories may surface that you haven't been aware of for years. As these feelings and memories emerge, you may feel worse before you feel better. Without a clear vision of potential benefits, it may be difficult to tolerate this emotional turmoil without shutting down or reverting to previous strategies to push away feelings.

Getting in touch with early memories can help you identify the strategies you developed to survive the abuse. Some of these strategies may be interfering with your work and intimate relationships as an adult. When you push away painful feelings, you cut off your awareness of joy, excitement, and enthusiasm as well. By becoming aware of how you were affected by the abuse, you can make conscious choices about your current behavior. Instead of shutting down or becoming depressed, you gain access to the full range of your emotional life as an adult.

Gay Men and Feelings

Men are socialized to be in control and not allow themselves to be emotionally vulnerable. It's considered all right for us to feel angry, but we're not supposed to admit feelings such as sadness, hurt, or fear. Men also tend to rationalize their feelings—they decide that there's no point in feeling upset or that they're not going to let something bother them, so they refuse to acknowledge their true emotional response. Keeping a stiff upper lip can keep you from crying, but you may get depressed instead.

Boys are ridiculed severely by other males for crying, for being afraid, or for seeking comfort. If we don't conform to these expectations, we may be ostracized for not "being a man." *Real emotional strength does not derive from denying your feelings, but from being able to feel without harming others or acting self-destructively.*

Some gay men developed coping strategies that helped them survive a traumatic childhood but which may interfere with expressing feelings as an adult. For example, cutting off feelings of hurt and sadness may have kept us from being harassed and humiliated, but suppressing these feelings can become such an automatic response that we may no longer be aware of them. Even if we realize that it's all right for men to cry, it's not that easy to get in touch with our hurt or sadness. We may cut off our emotions as a self-preserving reflex; yet those feelings are still there. As long as we continue to push them away, they are likely to express themselves through self-defeating behavior.

Similarly, we may have suppressed our desire for love and affection from other males to avoid ridicule and assault. As adults, we may accept that we are gay and pursue sexual contact, but it may still be difficult for us to express emotional vulnerability in intimate relationships. Becoming more aware of your feelings will increase your capacity for emotional intimacy.

How Feelings Work

Knowing something about feelings can help you feel more relaxed when they wash over you. You're not going to completely lose control or make a fool out of yourself just because you're in touch with your emotions. Instead of thinking of emotions as a threat to be avoided, you can begin to see them as allies in recovery. Below are ten points exploring how feelings operate in our lives.

1. Feelings are a form of natural healing.
2. Feelings are not permanent. They often shift once they are acknowledged.
3. You don't have to justify feelings.
4. Current feelings may relate to past situations.
5. Unacknowledged feelings tend to leak out in self-destructive behavior.
6. You don't have to act on your feelings.
7. Anger often masks hurt, sadness, or fear.

8. Boredom and restlessness may be clues to underlying feelings.
9. Unacknowledged feelings can result in physical symptoms.
10. You are more likely to get in touch with feelings in a supportive environment.

Let's look at each one of these ideas in more detail.

1. Feelings are a form of natural healing. Feelings can be seen as a form of emotional feedback. The response to a painful stimulus may include a physical as well as a mental adjustment: You have a rush of adrenalin with a fight or flight response, or you may laugh, yawn, or cry as a discharge of emotional tension. Allowing yourself to feel your emotions can help you heal from previous as well as current trauma. It also helps you regain your emotional equilibrium and think more clearly about what you want to do in response to a situation.

2. Feelings are not permanent. They often shift once they are acknowledged. We often try to distract ourselves from our feelings. However, the more you push away feelings, the more pressing they become. You may think that once you succumb to the feeling, you will always feel that way. Although feelings press for acknowledgment, they do not last forever. They often change once you recognize them.

3. You don't have to justify feelings. We are responsible for what we *do,* but we don't have to control or justify how we *feel.* Knowing that feelings arise spontaneously, you don't need to put yourself down for having feelings that you can't explain. You are more likely to discover why you feel anger, fear, or sadness when you allow yourself to feel your emotions. Although feelings are nonrational, they usually make sense in some way.

4. Current feelings may relate to past situations. When feelings arise that don't seem to fit the present moment, you may be able to relate them to the past. You don't need to discount your feelings just because they seem out of proportion to the current stimulus. Instead, see them as clues to previous hurt. What does this feeling remind you of? Rather than avoiding or fleeing any situation that makes you uncomfortable, it may be useful to face that discomfort so that you can discover the source of a particular emotional response.

5. Unacknowledged feelings tend to leak out in self-destructive behavior. Ignoring or discounting feelings doesn't make them go away. Instead, they tend to leak out through self-defeating behavior. How you behave is often a clue to how you feel, so you can get in touch with feelings by looking at what you do. Being late for work every day, avoiding sex with your partner, or becoming sarcastic with friends may be clues to underlying feelings. You also gain more control over compulsive behavior by recognizing the feelings that motivate habitual responses.

6. You don't have to act on your feelings. Recognizing how you feel doesn't mean that you have to act in a certain way. You actually have *more* choices when you are in touch with your feelings, because they are not pressing for acknowledgment. You gain more control over what used to be an automatic response. For example, a severe disappointment doesn't mean that you have to have a drink; if you're attracted to someone, you don't have to have sex immediately; and just because you're angry with your lover doesn't mean that you have to leave him. Once you acknowledge your feelings, you can choose how (or whether) to express them in a given situation. Instead of having a drink, call a friend and talk about your disappointment; instead of having sex right away, ask someone out; instead of walking out on your lover or being verbally abusive, say how you feel, assert your own needs, and negotiate a mutually acceptable solution.

7. Anger often masks hurt, sadness, or fear. It may be easier for men to feel angry than it is to get in touch with underlying feelings of hurt, sadness, or fear. In a conflict with a partner, for example, you may feel hurt or afraid, but you may express anger because you feel too vulnerable to admit your sadness or hurt. Notice your anger patterns. Are you feeling something besides anger in these situations?

8. Boredom and restlessness may be clues to underlying feelings. A lot of men have trouble getting in touch with feelings in the beginning of recovery. They feel bored and restless. They miss the level of stimulation they got from drugs or compulsive behavior. Society reinforces our tendency to keep ourselves busy and push away feelings. We may distract ourselves from our feelings by going out, watching TV, having sex, or taking drugs.

While there's nothing wrong with idle diversions, you don't always have to be entertained. Sometimes just sitting with boredom and restlessness may uncover other feelings. You may be holding on to resentments that you hesitate to speak up about, or you may realize that you are holding yourself back from your true interests. Instead of distracting yourself from boredom, use your discontent to assert yourself in your relationships or to pursue work that really interests you.

9. Unacknowledged feelings can result in physical symptoms. When you don't acknowledge your feelings, they may express themselves through tension headaches, backaches, digestive problems, ulcers, or other physical ailments. Many men are not aware of the amount of tension they hold in their neck and shoulders. They may ignore physical complaints until they become seriously incapacitated. Exercise and massage can help alleviate physical tension and release underlying feelings.

10. You are more likely to get in touch with feelings in a supportive environment. Feelings tend to emerge with friends who can listen to you, accept your feelings, and empathize with you. Empathic listeners demonstrate their caring by their willingness to hear us and acknowledge the profound impact of our pain, even if it's outside the realm of their experience. They do so without immediately trying to offer advice, make us feel better, or talk us out of feeling bad.

Once you feel the freedom to be in touch with your emotions, whatever they are, your sense of self-worth is not as vulnerable to each passing feeling. You begin to accept yourself rather than trying to live up to others' expectations of who you should be. Self-acceptance allows you to break through the cycle of shame.

Grieving for Your Lost Childhood

If you were abused as a child, it probably wasn't safe to express your feelings of fear, hurt, and rage. These feelings may reemerge in the course of recovery, especially during psychotherapy. As you acknowledge the ways in which you were neglected or abused, you may experience a profound sense of loss. You are essentially grieving for your own lost childhood—the lack of a carefree and nonabusive home; the loss of innocence, if you were sexually abused; and missing out on the experience of being loved, nurtured, and accepted for who you were.

Some gay men mourn the lack of a family that could have acknowledged and supported their sexual orientation, especially when they still lived at home. Although some families are able finally to appreciate us for who we are, others never come around. It can be very painful to have it finally sink in that your parents' love was dependent on your willingness to fulfill a certain image for their own needs. Realizing that you can't compel anyone to love you can also be a relief, however. When you give up trying to influence your parents' feelings, you can allow yourself to grieve that loss and begin to heal.

One reason why sadness may be hard to acknowledge is that it reminds us of feeling humiliated by other males. Some of us learned to protect ourselves by not showing our hurt and sadness. We didn't want to give our tormentors the satisfaction of having gotten to us. Unfortunately, we probably lost either way—if we cried, we were ridiculed, but if we pretended not to be hurt, we shut ourselves off from our emotions.

You may get to the point where you recognize your anger toward rejecting parents, but it may still be difficult to feel the underlying grief. Getting in touch with sorrow over being abused may remind you of your vulnerability as a child. You may associate your feelings of fear, hurt, and humiliation with being dependent on them for approval. As an adult, you're safe now, and you don't need their approval anymore. You no longer have to shut down your emotional response to the rejection and abuse you suffered when you were younger.

You also may resist grieving for hostile and rejecting parents if you feel that you're better off without them. However, you're not really grieving for them; your grief is for the lack of nurturing parents who could have loved and accepted you as you really are. Allowing yourself to feel your sadness and hurt will help you heal from an emotionally abusive childhood. Healing from past hurt will help you become more emotionally available in your relationships as an adult.

Gaining Access to Sadness

Most men learn very early how to keep themselves from crying. We do this by tensing our muscles and holding our breath. It may become such an automatic response that you're not aware of doing it, so it's difficult to cry even if you want to. A simple way to learn how to cry is to go to sad movies. Some men feel foolish crying at a sentimental scene or song, but it's not really the movie that we are crying for. When we allow ourselves to identify with the character on the screen, we're crying for some loss or wish that was never fulfilled in our own lives. Watching a sad movie can help us get in touch with our own feelings.

You also might want to look at childhood photographs, listen to children's stories, and read accounts of other people's progress in recovery. Some men find it very helpful to visit the town and see the house where they spent their earliest years. Hearing the stories of other men in support groups is an excellent way to gain more access to your own feelings.

The next time you find yourself choking up at a movie or a story, just observe what you do. Notice how you constrict the muscles in your throat and hold your breath. For most men this is an automatic response. Don't be harsh with yourself or put yourself down. Just notice how you stop yourself. You have already gotten in touch with feeling moved by a poignant portrayal of another person's feelings.

You may have noticed that it's difficult to talk when you're choking up with sadness. You may feel self-conscious about the tears welling up in your eyes, realizing that if you keep talking you'll start to cry. The reason you choke up is because you are trying to keep from crying. You can't cry without breathing, so you stop talking and hold your breath. If you keep talking about how you feel, you'll continue to breathe, which will help you relax the muscles that keep you from sobbing. Allow yourself to sob and feel your sadness. Tears begin to flow naturally.

When you allow yourself to cry, you may get in touch with earlier feelings of sadness or memories of being humiliated. You may not even be aware of why you are crying. You don't need to figure it out right now. Just keep breathing and let the feelings wash over you.

If you feel self-conscious crying at a theater, rent a videotape.

Watch it by yourself or with a friend who can gently remind you to keep breathing. You might want to hold on to a stuffed animal or ask your friend to hold you. As you expand your ability to feel for others, you may find that you're able to feel more emotion in response to events in your own life. You begin to heal from the hurt and sadness that you experienced as a vulnerable child, and you gain more access to your feelings as an adult.

Feeling Overwhelmed

The recovery process can be uneven. You may feel confident on some days and then feel exhausted, moody, or depressed for no apparent reason. Feelings and memories may be stimulated by listening to news reports about child abuse, hearing other people's stories, interacting with your family, reading recovery books, and going to your support groups. Getting in touch with feelings is a major part of recovery, but you don't want to be so flooded with emotional turmoil that you are incapable of functioning in your daily life. It's important to find a balance between allowing yourself to feel and not being overwhelmed. If you know how your emotions work, you can avoid feeling panicked by them. Reaching out to others can also help you feel less overwhelmed.

Panic Attacks

Forgotten memories can be pretty frightening when they reemerge. Panic attacks may occur in response to being flooded with feelings. You get a rush of adrenalin that charges you with a fight or flight response. This feeling of extreme physical arousal becomes a signal that something is terribly wrong, which panics you, and you get another jolt of adrenalin. A vicious cycle sets in as your physiological response reinforces a catastrophic mind-set, and your panic pumps even more adrenalin into your system. You may have trouble breathing, you may be afraid that you're having a heart attack, or you may feel as if you are about to die. Some people hyperventilate until they get cramps in their hands and feet, which frightens them even more.

If you put a paper bag (*not* a plastic bag) over your nose and mouth, you will be able to regain the proper mixture of carbon dioxide in your bloodstream. You stop sweating, feel less faint, and the cramping goes away. You can also take slow, shallow breaths, and try to relax. If you have trouble relaxing, you may want to take a brisk walk to use up some of the adrenalin.

It helps to remind yourself that you are caught in a vicious circle. You may be able to break this cycle by altering the thoughts that are keeping you upset. For example, if you had a memory that you were molested as a child, you may become very agitated over whether to confront your parents and what might happen if you did so. You can remind yourself that it will take a while to sort through your feelings, and you don't have to decide what to do right at that moment.

It's hard to remember reassuring thoughts when you are in the midst of a panic attack. It's important to seek support when you feel flooded by feelings, memories, or nightmares. Call someone who can give you the support you need: a friend, your sponsor, or a crisis line. You can also write down all your thoughts so that they'll stop whirling around in your mind.

Some people get in touch with suicidal impulses during panic attacks (see chapter 10). It takes a while to learn how to deal with feelings of terror, rage, and hurt in a way that keeps you safe and doesn't put you in jeopardy of harming anyone else. The idea is not to talk yourself out of your feelings, but to stop the cycle of catastrophic thinking that leads to panic. Reassuring thoughts might include the following: "You're panicking right now because you're very upset. Your job right now is to be in touch with feelings without jumping to conclusions. You don't have to solve this problem right now." Allow yourself to cry and shake and sob. If you have cramps, breathe into a paper bag (*not* a plastic bag). Gradually slow down your breathing and see if you can relax. Go for a brisk walk. Call a friend, your sponsor, or a crisis line and talk about your feelings. If you continue to obsess about a matter that you can't do anything about, you might want to engage in some other activity to stop the obsession: get some exercise, read a book, go to a movie with a friend. To calm yourself in future attacks, write down these reminders and other insights that have reassured you in the past and keep the list in your wallet.

Panic attacks may be related to forgotten memories and can be a clue to earlier abuse. However, some people have panic attacks that don't appear to be connected with any particular event in their lives. This kind of panic attack may be caused by a chemical imbalance and should be evaluated by a psychiatrist. This condition often responds well to small doses of antidepressant medication combined with psychotherapy.[1]

Depression

Depression isn't so much a feeling as it is a response to the blockage of feelings. Depression often results from internalized anger, unacknowledged sadness, or pessimistic beliefs about your prospects for the future. Instead of counting your blessings, putting yourself down, or trying to talk yourself out of being depressed, you can use your depression as a clue to underlying emotions. If you have bouts of depression that last longer than a few days, you may want to seek psychotherapy to help you work through these feelings. Listed below are some common sources and types of depression. We will provide some suggestions for getting at the emotions that underlie the depression for each source.

- Unacknowledged grief
- Initial stages of recovery from substance abuse
- Anger turned inward
- Negative beliefs
- Chemical imbalance

Unacknowledged grief. Our culture tends to reinforce a stoic response to emotional devastation, especially in men. Unacknowledged grief, however, can lead to depression.[2]

Expressing sorrow is a healthy response to any major loss: the breakup of a relationship, a friend moving away, not getting the job we want, a serious illness, or an injury. As mentioned earlier, you may grieve for your own lost childhood or feel sad about an estrangement from your family. Even changes that you looked forward to, such as graduation or retirement, can involve the loss of familiar faces and routines.

When the enormity of the loss sinks in, you may feel sad and melancholy. Former interests pale, and daily tasks can feel burdensome. It helps to reach out to others for support. Talk about how important this person or job was to you, how much the illness or injury will interfere with your plans, or how your change of role or status has affected you. With the death of a lover or close friend, a memorial service can be an important time for acknowledging the profound nature of your loss. You can also get together with a friend to talk about what you miss most about your loved one. You might want to share photographs, letters, or memories of your life together to facilitate your grief. Allow yourself to be held by a friend, and let yourself feel your sadness over how much you miss the times you had together.

Initial stages of recovery from substance abuse. If you have been using drugs or compulsive behavior to ward off feelings, you may crash after withdrawal. Some drugs, such as crack cocaine, stimulate the dopamine in the brain toward a state of elation. Once the dopamine is depleted, you lose your natural capacity for pleasure. You are likely to become depressed during withdrawal from alcohol, speed, and cocaine addictions.

In early recovery, you are confronted with devastating feelings at a time when you have the least resources for coping with them. Shame and self-hatred may be mixed with hopelessness and depression. It may be difficult to maintain a vision of what's possible through the process of healing. The temptation is strong to fall back in with friends who are still using. You need support to tolerate the onrush of feelings that you managed to push away over many years. You may gain confidence in the process of recovery by seeing the improvement of others in your program and by getting feedback about your own progress.

Anger turned inward. If you were abused as a child, you may not feel safe acknowledging the anger and sorrow you feel toward those who abused you. You may feel guilty for betraying the family secret, or you may feel ashamed of what happened to you even though it wasn't your fault that you were abused. Because your parents treated you badly, you may have internalized the message that there was something essentially wrong with you. Depression may result from turning your anger on yourself. You may blame yourself for having post-traumatic symptoms, for not getting your life together, or for holding yourself back from your true interests. Self-blame makes it difficult to do anything to improve your situation (see section on Mobilizing Anger, below).

Negative beliefs. Almost everyone gets depressed at times. Depression may pass within a few hours or a couple of days, but for some people it can be so debilitating that it perpetuates itself: You don't feel much like doing anything, so you withdraw from pleasurable activities. Withdrawal and isolation constrict your environment, so you have little outside stimulation. With nothing to look forward to, you may develop negative beliefs about your prospects for improvement. These beliefs can give rise to a self-fulfilling prophecy: You don't expect your situation to change, so you don't do anything to change it. In chapter 10, we will challenge some of the distortions in thinking that result in unrealistic conclusions and reinforce depression.

Chemical imbalance. Some people seem to have a chemical imbalance that results in depression. They get depressed for no apparent reason. If you are depressed but have not suffered any losses or trauma that you are aware of, or if you haven't made any progress in therapy, you may want to be evaluated by a psychiatrist for antidepressant medication. Antidepressants don't make you high, but they can take the edge off your depression so that you can mobilize yourself for more rewarding activities.[3]

The forms of depression outlined above are not mutually exclusive. You may have suffered a major loss, but then also withdraw and come to negative conclusions about your prospects for the future. You may be reacting to early abuse, but also suffer from a chemical imbalance that might respond to medication. You may be in the early stages of recovery and also turn your anger on yourself. It takes a while to sort through all the possible combinations that could be influencing your depression. Psychotherapy can be an important resource for handling prolonged bouts of depression. As you work through your underlying feelings, you gradually increase your capacity for involvement with new interests. Some people find that getting involved with some project outside of themselves gives them a sense of meaning and purpose. Caring for children, volunteering for an AIDS organization, or assisting older people can provide connection with others, new perspectives, and something to look forward to.

Mobilizing Anger for Positive Change

Once you stop turning anger inward through depression or self-destructive behavior, you are likely to get in touch with intense feelings of anger and rage toward perpetrators of past abuse as well as toward those who continue to oppress you. Some men learned while growing up that anger was dangerous. They associate it with the abuse they suffered, and they don't want to be anything like their perpetrators. They have seen how anger can perpetuate itself through a vicious circle of spiteful retaliation.

Anger does not have to be self-destructive or injurious to others. You can use your anger to assert your rights, set appropriate limits to abusive behavior, and mobilize yourself to call friends and go to support groups.

It's helpful to externalize your anger so you don't obsess about it, feel paralyzed, or turn it inward and blame yourself: pound a mattress; shout (into a pillow, if you need to muffle the noise); write it down or draw it; punch clay, or dig into the earth; run, swim, do martial arts and other sports. You can also use your anger to lift yourself out of depression by getting involved with organizations that counter the effects of homophobia and abuse in the wider society: AIDS, homelessness, ecology, or other causes that attract your interest.

Pacing Yourself

The reason you may have suppressed feelings in the first place is that it wasn't safe to express them, so you are likely to feel some anxiety when you go against this prohibition. The transition from avoiding feelings to conscious awareness can be difficult and painful, but it can also be exhilarating and freeing.

Survivors of early abuse often vacillate between elation and despair. You finally get a clear idea that recovery from a painful childhood is truly possible, and then crash when you confront the reality of slogging through the daily hardships that get in your way. You may feel heartened by a sense of community in your support group, but then be discouraged by the difficulty of connecting with other gay men. You may fall in love, but then be faced with the conflicts that arise in any relationship.

Realizing that the process of healing has its ups and downs can help you tolerate feelings without blaming yourself or giving up. When you take things "one day at a time," you are less likely to despair or to return to self-defeating behavior in the face of disappointment. It takes practice to catch yourself in self-defeating patterns. Knowing that progress is uneven can help you be patient with yourself and anticipate setbacks as normal events. If you get caught up in feelings of shame, identify the early source of these feelings. You no longer need to be controlled by the messages of low self-worth you may have internalized from your family.

You may feel especially vulnerable during times of stress, such as when starting a new job, moving, taking an HIV test, or finding out that a friend is infected with HIV. Instead of isolating yourself from others, make sure you reach out even more assertively for support. Increase your attendance at meetings and call your friends to talk about your feelings.

Given the current health crisis for gay men, it may be difficult to pace yourself. Don't use the urgency of caring for others as a way to escape from your own feelings. Take care of others, but take care of yourself, too. Build some time-outs into your schedule. Even a short break can help you get back in touch with yourself—a walk by the water, a day out in the country, a movie, or just getting together with a friend.

Recovery can seem like a massive task. It helps to remember that you can't accomplish everything at once. Addictive and compulsive patterns are strong habits that may leave you feeling out of control at times; disappointments may trigger old "tapes" and negative messages. Change is gradual and incremental, establishing itself bit by bit over a long period of time. You don't need to blame yourself or assume that something is wrong when you have setbacks or feel depressed once in a while. Rather than getting down on yourself when you act self-destructively, simply recognize that you slipped, and reaffirm your desire to stay with this process. Having a number of resources for support will help you cope with disappointment without getting caught in another cycle of self-defeating behavior.

During the course of recovery, you will gradually increase your ability to pay attention to feelings, identify your usual reaction, and change your behavior. Healing from past abuse is not all heavy and painful. Feeling your emotions may seem difficult at first, but you often feel better afterward. You learn that avoiding feelings causes far more pain than releasing them. As you experience the full range of your emotions, you can expect moments of lightness and humor, empowering insights, and a great deal of relief about not having to pretend anymore.

Instead of escaping from feelings, you begin to welcome your emotions as a sign that you are alive. As you get in touch with your feelings, you may also become more conscious of the negative messages you absorbed during your childhood. These may still influence your self-image and how you feel about yourself as an adult. In the next chapter, we will look at various ways to challenge these negative messages and replace them with self-nurturing encouragement.

Relating These Ideas to Your Own Experience

- Look over the list of how feelings work. How is your own emotional life different from this description? How is it the same?
- How were you treated as a boy when you felt sad? When was the last time you cried? Are there any situations now in which you feel comfortable expressing your sadness?
- Who in your life do you feel comfortable enough to call when you feel sad, depressed, or angry?

- The next time you feel depressed, see if you can get in touch with any underlying feelings of anger, hurt, or sadness.
- What was your experience with anger while you were growing up? How would you like to deal with your anger now?

Awareness of Feelings Exercise

The following exercise can help you gain more access to your feelings. It will also help you develop your self-awareness. By gently observing your thoughts and feelings from one moment to the next, you will have a direct experience of the transient nature of your emotions. You become less judgmental toward your failings and more accepting of your natural growth. You will increase your ability to make conscious choices rather than immediately acting on your impulses.

▼

Sit in a comfortable chair with your arms and legs uncrossed. Start out by saying "Now I'm aware of . . ." and then fill in the blank. Let your eyes move around the room: Now I'm aware of the chair. Now I'm aware of the window. Now I'm aware of the lamp. Now I'm aware of the rug. Go all the way around the room, just noticing what attracts your attention, repeating the same pattern: Now I'm aware of the picture on the wall. Now I'm aware that I'm sitting here in this chair.

Come back to yourself and become aware of the sounds you hear: Now I'm aware of hearing the bird outside the window. Now I'm aware of the car driving past the house. Move on to physical sensations: Now I'm aware of my legs against the chair. Now I'm aware of feeling warm. Now I'm aware that my throat is dry.

Then move into thoughts, memories, and emotions: Now I'm aware of wondering how long this exercise is going to last. Now I'm aware of some fear about what I might discover. Now I'm aware of . . . feeling blank. Now I'm aware of being bored. Now I'm aware of feeling hungry. Now I'm aware of what I want to fix for lunch. Now I'm aware that I'm trying to escape from this exercise. Now I'm aware of feeling sad. Now I'm aware that I don't know why I'm sad. Now I'm aware of thinking it's silly to feel sad if I don't know what I'm sad about. Now I'm aware of judging myself. Now I'm aware that it's all right to feel whatever I'm feeling. Now I'm aware that I often felt like I had to justify my feelings to my mother. Now I'm aware . . .

▲

Try this for yourself. Speaking out loud will help you keep from drifting. It also helps to have someone listen to you to keep you focused. You may find that you edit less of your awareness when you do this exercise by yourself or with a therapist. You can also just acknowledge that you are editing your awareness: "Now I'm aware that I'm choosing not to say what I'm aware of." The focus of this exercise is on your own awareness, not on self-revelation.

The first time you do this exercise, try it for just two or three minutes. Over the next few days, gradually increase the time to ten or fifteen minutes. You can also try this as a writing exercise: Put "Now I'm aware of . . ." at the top of a column, then write a word or two on each line. After the exercise, you may want to write down whatever reactions, feelings, or memories you had in response to this experience. If you would like to share any insights, bring it to your support group or therapy session.

If you keep at this exercise over a period of weeks and months, you may find that your jumble of thoughts and feelings becomes less agitated over time. You may want to let go of the reminder "Now I'm aware of . . ." and simply watch with a gentle awareness as your breath moves in and out, your stomach rises and falls. When you become aware of a memory, an image, or a feeling, just make a mental note of it—"Now I'm aware of . . ."—and then return to your breath. You may find over time that the turbulent storm of your emotions gradually settles into a calm pool, with occasional ripples of thoughts and feelings.[4]

10

▼

Self-Nurturing

In this chapter we will look at distortions in thinking that can interfere with progress in recovery. You will learn how to differentiate feelings from unrealistic conclusions and how to challenge the hurtful messages you may have absorbed as a child. By replacing these negative messages with affirmations of your true abilities, you can provide the nurturing for yourself that you may never have received from your own family.

Distortions in Thinking

Some people get stuck in a cycle of negative beliefs that leaves them depressed because they don't see any options for improving their lives.

Listed below are common distortions in thinking that can lead to un-realistic beliefs and negative conclusions about your prospects for change.[1]

- Perfectionism
- All-or-nothing thinking
- The tyranny of "should"
- Limiting yourself with a label
- Ignoring the positive and exaggerating the negative
- Overgeneralizing
- Taking things personally
- Anticipating the worst
- Comparing yourself to others

Perfectionism. As a child, you may have gotten the message that you could never do anything right, which left you with the belief that if you didn't do something perfectly, you were a failure. No one is perfect; everyone makes mistakes. Rather than experiencing mistakes as a confirmation of your unworthiness, you can learn from your mistakes and use them as feedback for making improvements.

Throughout this book are many suggestions for feeling better about yourself. Don't assume that you have to do a perfect job of recovery! It takes a lot of support, practice, and perseverance to learn new ways to deal with feelings and counter the negative messages that you may have internalized as a child.

All-or-nothing thinking. Closely related to perfectionism, all-or-nothing thinking can lead to giving up if you're rejected, disappointed, or if you can't do something right the very first time. For example, if you have a slip in recovery from substance abuse, it doesn't mean that you might as well give up. If you're rejected by someone for insisting on safer sex, it doesn't mean that others will also reject you for being safe. Feeling sad or hurt is a normal response to disappointment, but you needn't conclude that you're never going to have an intimate relationship on the basis of this one experience, or even if you have had several disappointments.

The tyranny of "should." The word *should* implies a sense of obligation. There are a lot of mundane things everyone needs to take care of to function in the world, but you gain more control (and feel less resentment) by changing your "shoulds" into conscious choices. The recognition that you are constantly making active choices can also help you assess whether your standards or values are realistic. Here are some examples.

"I should work harder." Work harder for what? Is it worth it to you to miss out on the free time you already enjoy? If not, adjust your standards. If you decide that you *want* to work harder for a specific goal, then change the "should" to acknowledge this desire: "I'm working really hard so I can complete this project, finish school, and take a nice vacation."

"I should lose weight." Says who? What would losing weight mean in terms of how you feel about yourself? Are you willing to change how you eat and get more exercise? If not, adjust your expectation about how much weight you would like to lose. If it's worth it to you, change the "should" to match your desire: "I want to get in shape so I can enjoy more physical activities." Then get the support you need to follow through on your plan.

"I shouldn't have called my partner a jerk." You don't gain much by punishing yourself or berating yourself with "shoulds." Instead, you can accept that you're a fallible human being and make amends where appropriate. You can also identify the behavior that led to your frustration, say how you feel about it, and negotiate an acceptable solution.

"I should call Aunt Cecile for her birthday." What's the conflict? Whenever you call Cecile she asks when you're going to get married. You don't want to come out to her, but you're tired of lying. Yet you'd feel guilty if you didn't call. By identifying all of these elements, you are more likely to come up with a decision that you can live with, instead of feeling resentful or "forgetting" to call, and then feeling guilty:

"I don't want to call Cecile, so I'll send her a card instead."

"I'll tease her by asking 'When are *you* getting married?' "

"I'm tired of pretending, so I'll come out."

Whenever you tell yourself that you should or shouldn't be doing something, you burden yourself with unnecessary guilt and resentment. Instead of making some improvement, you're likely to continue with self-defeating behavior by rebelling against the tyranny of "should." Switching your shoulds into choices will help you clarify what you really want.

Limiting yourself with a label. When you label yourself as being dumb or lazy or too dependent, you box yourself in. Identifying behaviors instead of labeling yourself will help you recognize underlying feelings. Understanding your feelings will also help you identify your "shoulds" and make new choices. The label of "I'm too shy" could be changed to "I feel self-conscious at parties where I don't know anyone." The tyrannical "should" might be "I should be gregarious at all times." A more realistic choice might be to ask the host to introduce you to a couple of people.

Ignoring the positive and exaggerating the negative. Some abuse survivors ignore the gradual changes that they actually have made in their lives. They don't appreciate their real accomplishments, talents, and interests. Instead they tend to focus on faults or imperfections and find it difficult to accept compliments. If they felt manipulated as a child, they may be suspicious of someone showing interest in them. See if you can accept a compliment by just saying "thank you." You deserve to feel nurtured and appreciated.

Overgeneralizing. When you use the words *never* or *always,* you may be overgeneralizing. You can challenge your generalizations by asking yourself whether you are really always in a hurry, or never on time; if you're always forgetful, or never remember anything. Underlying these generalizations may be unrealistic "shoulds": I should never be late; I should always remember everything. You can counter these by saying "It's important to me to be on time. If I'm running late, I can call ahead. Next time I'll give myself more time."

Taking things personally. Some people tend to experience other people's behavior as if it were intended as a personal affront. Parents who assume that their gay son became homosexual to spite them are a common example of this kind of thinking.

If someone doesn't return your phone call or write you back, you might assume it's because he doesn't want to. In the shifting world of gay dating patterns, it's sometimes difficult to tell whether or not an unreturned call is intended personally. Sometimes no reply *is* a reply, but people also mislay letters or messages, forget that you called, or become distracted by other events and emotional pulls in their lives. Your friend might also have a hard time being direct about what he wants, but you can describe your own expectation about returning calls and find out his.

Anticipating the worst. Some people have a superstitious belief that you will bring bad luck upon yourself if you exult too much in your good fortune. They guard against hopefulness by reminding themselves of the doom and gloom that are very likely to follow. They try to ward off misfortune by anticipating the worst, but their negative predictions may become a self-fulfilling prophecy: They tell themselves "I'm never going to meet anyone," so they never go out and get to know other people. You will increase your chances of meeting someone, getting a good job, or finding a decent place to live by identifying your goals and developing a concrete plan of action.

Comparing yourself to others. There will always be someone handsomer, richer, younger, thinner, or more successful than you. There is no reason to assess your essential worth as a human being by comparing yourself to anyone else. We all have unique experiences, views, and special qualities. If you find that some people remind you of neglected interests, you can use your admiration to inspire the development of your own latent talents. As we age or when we are faced with serious illness, we may not be as productive as we once were, but our worth is not dependent on our productivity. We are worthwhile simply because we exist.

How Thoughts Influence Feelings

Many self-help books promote the idea that particular events don't cause emotional reactions; rather, it's our beliefs about these events that lead us to feel bad.[2] They say, for example, that being caught in traffic doesn't cause anger; it's your belief that you shouldn't have to be held up that makes you angry. Here is the basic outline of this concept:

EVENT: Caught in traffic.
UNREALISTIC BELIEF: I can't stand being caught in traffic.
FEELING: Anger.

The idea is that if you change unrealistic beliefs, you will change how you feel about many of the events in your life: "I'm stuck in traffic, which is inconvenient, but I don't have to make myself angry. I can listen to music, or plan tomorrow's meeting." Unrealistic beliefs about how the world "should" work *can* make you miserable. If you alter your beliefs, you aren't as likely to make yourself upset. Countering unrealistic beliefs works pretty well with minor annoyances such as a flat tire or rain during a picnic. Having a flat tire is annoying, but it's not a disaster; instead of letting rain spoil your picnic, you can huddle in the car with your boyfriend.

The assumption that feelings are *primarily* caused by unrealistic beliefs, however, is misleading when we are confronted with a serious loss. It makes sense that you would feel sad, hurt, or afraid in response to a major loss, such as the breakup of a relationship, the death of a friend, or a positive HIV test. When you try to convince yourself that you feel bad because you have some irrational beliefs, you can end up repressing your feelings rather than allowing yourself to grieve.

Similarly, post-traumatic symptoms are a natural response to trauma. Well-meaning but ignorant friends of early abuse survivors sometimes try to convince them that they should be over it by now. Why still be upset about something that happened a long time ago? Your family's minimization of childhood abuse also can undermine your ability to identify your feelings. Many survivors blame themselves for continuing to experience post-traumatic symptoms. Feelings in response to early trauma and major loss need to be recognized and worked through, not rationalized or repressed.

However, even with severe loss, thoughts can influence feelings. You may make yourself feel worse by jumping to negative conclusions about what your loss means. What we need is a balance between acknowledging feelings and challenging negative conclusions. In the following section, you will learn how to identify underlying emotions, counter unrealistic conclusions, and get support for taking action.

Feelings Versus Conclusions

In common speech, we often substitute conclusions for feelings. We say "I feel hopeless," when what we really mean is "I feel sad" or "I'm afraid about my prospects for the future." Hopelessness isn't really a feeling; it is a *conclusion* derived from the pain you feel and from your beliefs about future prospects. When you recognize the underlying sadness, you can grieve for your loss. It's possible to feel sad about a major loss without assuming that you will never get anywhere. Instead of shutting down, you can open yourself to new experiences and opportunities.

For example, if your partner leaves you, it makes sense that you would feel sad over the loss of a relationship. Your sadness isn't caused by an irrational belief; it's a normal reaction to a genuine loss of intimacy. However, you can make yourself feel even worse by jumping to a negative conclusion about what this loss means. Here's the outline of this pattern:

EVENT: Left by partner.
UNDERLYING FEELING: Sad.
NEGATIVE CONCLUSION: I'm never going to find anyone else.
RESULT: Hopeless and depressed.

It can be a relief to acknowledge your sadness rather than trying to talk yourself out of your pain. However, when you tell yourself, "I'm never going to find anyone else," you are leaping to a conclusion that leaves you few options. Despair prevents you from evaluating your prospects realistically. Instead of feeling the sadness and grieving, you shut down and become depressed.

When you experience a major disappointment, try to identify the underlying feeling—"I feel sad" or "I'm really hurt," or "I'm afraid." When you allow yourself to grieve your loss, you are more likely to gain some clarity about what to do next, instead of getting stuck in your negative conclusion. *It is possible to experience loss and disappointment without concluding that you are any less worthwhile as a person.*

Countering Unrealistic Conclusions

In addition to feeling the underlying emotion, you can also counter unrealistic conclusions with reminders of your true abilities. With the above example, the negative conclusion is "I'm never going to find anyone." The underlying feeling may be sadness, anger, or fear. Your true abilities include being able to reach out and meet new people. You can counter your negative conclusion by affirming that you really do have a lot of good qualities that can help you find someone new.

Here's an example of what you might say to yourself: "I'm really disappointed that this didn't work out. I feel sad and lonely, and I miss the good times we had together. After all these disappointments, I'm afraid I'll never find anyone. But I don't have to keep telling myself I'm never going to be in another relationship, because that will just keep me from meeting anyone new. I feel sad, and maybe I need to withdraw for a while, but eventually I'll be ready to reach out again and meet other men. Just because things didn't work out doesn't mean I'm not a worthwhile person, or that I don't deserve a loving partner. I have a lot of kind and loving qualities that I could bring to a new relationship."

Support

When you've had a major disappointment, it's not always easy to realize that you have jumped to an unrealistic conclusion. Negative conclusions may even help you get in touch with feelings of sorrow that relate to previous disappointments. There is no need to put yourself down for feeling sad, or even for assuming your situation is hopeless. Getting support can help you work through your feelings and identify any distortions in your thinking. Get suggestions for various ways to counter these negative assumptions with your true abilities.

Then you can examine possibilities for taking action to improve your situation.

Taking Action

Once you have allowed yourself to feel the underlying emotion and you have countered unrealistic conclusions, then you are ready to take some action. In the example above, you might go out with friends for a while, find new ways to enjoy being by yourself, and eventually meet new people and date again. It's helpful to have a friend or other supportive person acknowledge your efforts and continue to help you counter unrealistic conclusions and other negative messages that you may have internalized while growing up.

Suicidal Impulses

Suicide is an extreme example of a negative conclusion created by all-or-nothing thinking. When people are overwhelmed by loss and disappointment, they may jump to the conclusion that suicide is the *only* way out. They have fastened onto a solution before they have the chance to work through their feelings. Panic and despair can distort their perception about alternative ways to handle their problems.[3]

If your life has been severely affected by early trauma, you may decide that your situation is hopeless because you don't yet have the perspective to see that things really could get better. You are still experiencing the consequences of an overwhelming assault on your whole sense of self. Without a vision of what else might be possible through therapy or other support, you internalize the negative messages of early abuse. You assume that you will never get anywhere, because that's been your experience so far—or at least that's how it feels when you are in the depths of your despair.

If you have the impulse to kill yourself, it's essential that you call your therapist or a crisis line to talk about your feelings. An empathic response may allow you to gain some perspective on other options besides suicide. If you feel so shut down that you are not able to agree not to hurt yourself until your next appointment, you may need to be hospitalized for a short amount of time. Hospitalization for suicidal intent doesn't mean that you're ''crazy''; it's simply a time-out so you can be kept safe while you're feeling this way. Remember that even feelings of despair are not permanent. You can reach out for support and take one day at a time to work through your feelings.

Nurturing Your Own Child Self

When you receive enough love and understanding as a child, you develop confidence in your ability to heal from hurt. If you never had adequate nurturing while growing up, you may tend to look for it from others. We are social beings, and we all need a certain amount of external acknowledgment of our experience. That's why it's so important to reach out to others for support. However, no one can supply the kind of unconditional nurturing, acceptance, and love that you never received from your parents. You can learn how to provide some of this encouragement for yourself by becoming your own nurturing parent.

As mentioned earlier, it is intolerable as a small child to realize that the very person who is supposed to protect you is being abusive. It is less anxiety-provoking to assume that you deserved to be punished, so you tend to blame yourself for your own abuse. Self-blame and shame lead to the conclusion that you are undeserving of love and affection. In this section we will provide a method for countering the negative messages you may have absorbed from your family and suggest some ways to affirm your true abilities.

Refuting Negative Messages

Long after leaving home, you may still hear the voice of a critical parent inside your head. Frequently we say things to ourselves that would horrify us if we overheard them said to anyone else, especially to a child. You may have developed these habits of thought in response to the criticism you grew up with, but this voice may continue to monitor every activity with unnecessary harshness.

Don't blame yourself for having developed this voice. A part of you may have needed to identify with the aggressor to avoid abusive treatment as a child. Although negative messages are usually untrue, exaggerated, and overly punitive, they may have served some protective function during your childhood. It can be helpful to acknowledge this protective function so that you can find a more nurturing way to take care of yourself.

It takes practice to counter negative patterns; you will have to catch yourself again and again. When you hear that critical voice, just become aware of it: There's that critical voice again. Noticing the voice is a significant step toward liberating yourself from it. In chapter 8, we talked about expanding the moment between impulse and action by noticing the impulse and becoming aware of underlying feelings. You can also interrupt negative conclusions by becoming aware of your critical voice. Listed below are some steps you can take to replace the internal critic with a nurturing statement of your true abilities, along with several examples:

1. Notice the negative message
2. Recognize that you are putting yourself down
3. Get in touch with underlying feelings
4. Identify the distortion in thinking
5. Acknowledge the protection function of the message
6. Counter the negative message with your true abilities

Example I

1. Negative message: You're never going to get anywhere, so what's the point in going back to school?
2. Recognition: I'm giving myself a negative message.
3. Underlying feelings: I'm angry with myself for dropping out of college and I'm afraid of another failure.
4. Distortion in thinking: Overgeneralizing from past disappointments.
5. Protective function: To keep from being disappointed again.
6. True abilities: I dropped out of college when I had no idea of what I wanted to do. I can go back now and study what I'm really interested in.

Example II

1. Negative message: You're a failure.
2. Recognition: I'm aware that I'm putting myself down.
3. Underlying feeling: Sadness or disappointment.
4. Distortion in thinking: Perfectionism.
5. Protective function: To prevent humiliation.
6. True abilities: Sometimes I don't get the results I want, but I can always learn from my mistakes.

Example III

1. Negative message: You shouldn't be so spiteful.
2. Recognition: I'm aware that I'm putting myself down.
3. Underlying feeling: Anger.
4. Distortion in thinking: The tyranny of "should."
5. Protective function: To prevent being rejected for showing anger.
6. True abilities: It's all right to feel angry. Being angry doesn't mean that I'm spiteful. I can say how I feel and negotiate for what I want without alienating people.

Example IV

1. Negative message: You tested positive for HIV, so you'll never find a lover or have sex again.
2. Recognition: I'm aware that I'm limiting myself because of my HIV status.
3. Underlying feelings: Anger, sadness, fear.
4. Distortion in thinking: Anticipating the worst.
5. Protective function: Protection against being rejected.
6. True abilities: I can have sex and still be safe. There are a lot of men who are willing to be in a relationship with someone who is HIV positive. I can reach out for support from other men and find out how they've been dealing with this.

Example V

1. Negative message: You're too sensitive.
2. Recognition: I'm aware that I'm judging myself.

3. Underlying feeling: Hurt.
4. Distortion in thinking: Limiting yourself with a label.
5. Protective function: To avoid being hurt.
6. True abilities: It's great to be sensitive to my surroundings— that's what keeps me alive. I can also check out my perceptions to see whether they are accurate.

Example VI

1. Negative message: You've had unsafe sex with him before, so why bother with safer sex now?
2. Recognition: I'm aware that I'm trying to rationalize unsafe sex.
3. Underlying feeling: Anger at myself for previous unsafe sex.
4. Distortion in thinking: All-or-nothing thinking.
5. Protective function: To avoid having to take responsibility for my behavior.
6. True abilities: I know I made a mistake in not having safer sex before, but it's still important to have safer sex now.

Try using this model for identifying and countering some of your own negative or homophobic messages. You can develop compassion for your feelings even when you are upset with yourself. Noticing the critical voice is cause for celebration, not recrimination, because you have caught yourself instead of continuing your negative train of thought. Try to accept yourself even when you put yourself down: "You are such a dope. Why can't you ever. . . . Oh, here I am putting myself down. Well, at least I caught myself." Then allow yourself to feel the underlying sadness, hurt, or fear, and replace the put-down with a nurturing message about your true abilities: "It's okay to feel however I feel. I can still decide what I want to do about it."

You can also give the kid inside you his own voice—what would he like to say to all of those critical parent messages? Write it down or say it aloud to an empty chair, just to get out the resentments and longing that you have never expressed before.

How would you like to have been treated as a child? Give that childlike part of yourself the kind of encouragement you wish you had had when you were young. Imagine a hurt child putting himself down.

Empathize with his frustration and give him loving and soothing encouragement: "You're frustrated and mad, you're tired of trying, and you can't stand it when you put yourself down again. It makes sense that you feel frustrated, but you caught yourself this time, and that's great."

Affirmations

Affirmations are statements that help you develop some perspective about your true potential. They serve as reminders of your essential worth as a human being, no matter how disappointed you are with your present circumstances. Your self-worth does not depend on success, youth, wealth, or even good health. You may feel sad, hurt, or angry in response to loss or other disappointments, but that's no reason to put yourself down or assume that you are any less valuable as a person.

Affirmations are useful in challenging unrealistic conclusions, but they shouldn't be used to talk yourself out of your feelings. Feel your emotions, but don't jump to negative conclusions.

Affirmations can be used to:

- Affirm your self-worth and improve your self-concept
- Recognize your ability to handle difficult situations
- Encourage the development of qualities and skills
- Take care of yourself
- Have fun with your child self
- Appreciate yourself

Here are some examples of affirmations in each of the above categories:

Affirming self-worth. You can remind yourself of your own self-worth through positive suggestions:

I am a loving and sensitive gay man.
I am worthwhile simply because I exist.
As a child, I did the best I could to survive difficult circumstances.

I can love and nurture my own child self as I wish I had been cared for when I was a boy.

Handling difficult situations. You can give yourself encouragement to make it through tough situations:

I may feel tense here, but I can relax, listen, and try to understand what he's saying.

It's all right if I get defensive; I can ask him to listen to me until I feel calmer.

This is a tough deadline, but I can concentrate on one section at a time and not be overwhelmed by the entire task.

It's okay if I cry to express my pain. I can be in touch with my feelings without threatening anyone or becoming self-destructive.

I had a slip-up in my recovery process and I'm disappointed with myself, but that's no reason to give up. I need to reach out and get support to work through my feelings.

Developing qualities and skills. You can encourage yourself to make progress in areas that you would like to improve:

I feel nervous asking a question, but asking questions is a good way to learn.

I don't have to have all the answers; I can learn by participating.

I may get a negative reaction when I'm honest about my ignorance, but some people will appreciate the fact that I feel confident enough to admit it when I don't know something. It feels better to be honest than to have to pretend.

I can go back to school or get the training I need to pursue this line of work.

Taking care of yourself. You can take care of yourself by:

Eating healthy foods	Going to the dentist
Physical exercise	Finding a decent place to live
Getting plenty of rest	Recreation
Regular medical exams	Reaching out to friends

Having fun with your child self. You can do fun and childlike things to get in touch with your spontaneity, humor, and joy:

Play with children

Get a doll or a stuffed animal

Tell stories with puppets

Draw with crayons, play with clay, finger paint

Ride a bike, roller skate, ice skate

Jump rope, skip, hop, swing, slide, climb a tree

Make a snowman, a sandcastle, build a tree house

Decorate your house for a holiday

Have a birthday party

Read children's stories

Sing songs around a campfire, tell jokes, do silly skits

Appreciating yourself. You can also appreciate things about yourself:

I like my eyes.

I have a great sense of humor.

I have a wonderful smile.

I have an infectious laugh.

I can be playful and mischievous.

I'm really good at baseball, cooking, swimming, drawing, Ping Pong, poker, sewing, singing, fixing a car, playing the piano, decorating a room, imitating Bette Davis . . .

I'm a good listener.

I have a lot of patience.

I have some very close and loving friends.

Make a list of your own affirmations in the categories listed above. Write down any of the negative messages you tell yourself and set aside time to counter each one. *Don't leave negative messages unchallenged*! If you can't think of a way to counter one, take it to your support group or therapy session and get some suggestions. Leave affirmations around the house and carry them with you to remind yourself of your essential worthiness. Encourage yourself to find meaningful work and develop loving relationships. Have some fun with like-minded friends and delight in your own child self. Share affirmations with friends or your support group and get new ideas from their examples. Look through collections of affirmations and copy the ones that capture your attention. Keep developing your own.

Remember to use affirmations to counter negative thinking, not to dismiss feelings—you feel whatever you feel, then you affirm your self-worth and counter unrealistic conclusions.

The Cycle of Healing from Internalized Shame

In chapter 6, we talked about how the cycle of shame can perpetuate self-defeating behavior. By countering the negative messages you may have absorbed when you were a child, you begin to heal from internalized shame. The self-defeating cycle of shame can be replaced by a cycle of healing:

1. Self-nurturing messages
2. Reaching out for support and empathy
3. Development of an authentic self
4. Feeling your emotions and healing from past wounds
5. Increasing self-esteem and confidence

1. Self-nurturing messages. You can counter negative messages and replace them with encouraging affirmations. Self-nurturing includes loving and accepting your child self as well as your adult self.

2. Reaching out for support and empathy. When you get support from others, you can feel safe to say what really happened to you while you were growing up. As you increase your ability to trust, you'll expand your network of intimate friends. You will feel understood and appreciated for who you are.

3. Development of an authentic self. You can learn to identify whatever false selves and self-destructive behavior you developed to survive and to avoid feeling ashamed. You can trace nonproductive patterns to previous trauma and discover healthier options for current behavior. You no longer need to pretend to be something you're not just because other people might feel threatened by your thoughts and feelings.

4. Feeling your emotions and healing from past wounds. As you gain more access to your feelings, you can grieve for the losses you have experienced. You learn that you have the right to feel whatever you feel; feelings are simply a source of emotional feedback. As you heal from early trauma, you feel freed from the limitations you absorbed from your family.

5. Increasing self-esteem and confidence. As you become more accepting of the full range of your emotional life, you become more confident. You can sort through current sources of shame or conflict and make amends where appropriate. You can identify the feelings behind unrealistic conclusions, which will allow you to think more clearly about what you want to do.

As you recover from self-destructive behavior and low self-esteem, you can restore for yourself the unconditional acceptance that you never received from your parents. Self-acceptance leads to change and growth and helps you develop empathy and compassion for your own child self. You can allow your feelings to wash over you without having to justify them. You can be yourself, whoever you are, in each moment. You don't have to prove yourself to anyone. You are worthwhile simply because you are you. You can relax and trust the unfolding process of your natural growth.

Relating These Ideas to
Your Own Experience

Below are two suggestions for ways to contact your own child self to get in touch with his wishes and needs. Both of these exercises may evoke powerful memories, so you might want to have someone available to talk to about your feelings. You may also discover a number of new ways to nurture yourself.

▼

Write a letter to your child self. Remember what it was like for you as a child growing up in your family, realizing that you felt same-sex attractions, feeling alone and unsure of yourself? Write a letter to your own child self. Tell him what you understand now about what he was going through. Ask him what he needs from you to feel better about himself. Write a letter back to yourself as that small child, expressing all of his unmet wishes and needs. Now write to him again as an adult and provide him with the comfort and soothing messages that he missed as a child.

A childhood exploration. If you have gaps in your memory of childhood, consider visiting the house or apartment where you grew up. If you're not able to go there (or if you would prefer not to), take a trip in your imagination: walk along your street and notice the houses of your neighbors. Who did you use to play with? What were their names? Can you see their faces? What was your favorite game with other kids in your neighborhood? When you reach your house, look at the yard, if you had one. Where did you play? Did you have a special place to hide? Walk around to the backyard. Scoot your feet through the leaves. Spin around and fall down in the grass and look up through the branches at the clouds moving overhead.

After a while, enter your house. How is the living room furnished? Where did you like to sit? What's on the walls? Go into the kitchen. What were your favorite smells? Walk down the hallway. Look into the bathroom and see the bathtub, the shower, the toilet, the sink. Walk by your parents' bedroom. Peek inside. What's on the dresser, the bed, hanging on the closet door? Find your bedroom. What's on the floor, the desk, the dresser, your bed? Look inside the closet. Find your favorite toy and play with it on the floor. If you had a stuffed animal, hug it close to you on your bed. Where did you feel comfortable in this house? Where did you feel afraid? What happened in these rooms?

Imagine yourself entering the bedroom as an adult and comforting that little boy. Hold him in your lap and rock him in your arms. Rest your cheek on top of his head. Ask him what he needs, what he really wants, what would help him feel protected, loved, and nurtured. Remind him that he is safe now, that you love him and you will take care of him, and that you will always be with him.

▲

11

▼

Seeking Support

Some gay men who were abused as children or who have suffered homophobic attacks do not get involved with substance abuse or compulsive behavior, yet they may still suffer from post-traumatic symptoms such as low self-esteem, depression, underachievement, self-deprivation, and codependency. This chapter will describe various resources for expanding your network of support. It will also give you an idea of what to expect in a therapy group for male survivors of dysfunctional families and childhood abuse.

Self-Help

In addition to twelve-step recovery groups dealing with addictive and compulsive behavior, there are also twelve-step programs designed to help you deal with dysfunctional families. These include Al-Anon for people who are family members or partners of an alcoholic; ACA, or Adult Children of Alcoholics; CODA, or Codependents Anonymous; and ISA, or Incest Survivors Anonymous.

Other self-help groups that do not use the twelve-step model of AA are also available all over the country for anyone who wants the support of people who are dealing with similar issues (see Appendix II). Some gay men have formed their own reading and consciousness-raising groups, weekend retreats, and informal support networks among friends. Some of their activities include telling stories, sharing writing, drawing, movement, and theater games. These groups help their members gain greater access to feelings, provide a safe place for feedback, and create a community of mutual support.

Friends and Lovers

Many of the benefits of group support can be developed within your own circle of friends. Some men hesitate to reach out to friends or to their lover because they don't want them to feel obligated, but it's helpful to remember that asking for what you want is not a demand. Tell your friend that you want him to say no if he's not available to support you in a particular way. Be specific about what you are asking for: You'd like him to come to a meeting with you, to talk on the phone, to hold you while you cry, or to listen to you once a week for a certain length of time. Let him know that it helps just to talk to someone about what you are going through; you don't expect him to solve your problem or make you feel better. By making requests of a number of friends, you can spread out your need for support and take care of yourself without overburdening your relationships. You might ask what you could do for them in return. Once you clarify your expectations, friends may become your most trusted allies in the process of recovery.

Some men find it more acceptable to acknowledge physical ailments than to talk about emotional pain. We visit someone in the hospital if he has had an accident, an operation, or an opportunistic infection from AIDS, but we tend to think that there is something wrong with us if we suffer from depression, hypervigilance, or other post-traumatic symptoms. We need and deserve just as much attention for recovery from emotional trauma as from accidents or illnesses.

If your friends feel overwhelmed by your needs, don't blame yourself. It's not your fault that you are suffering post-traumatic symptoms from early abuse. Nor does a friend's inability to meet some of your needs necessarily mean that he is rejecting you as a friend. He may be preoccupied with other concerns, or your story may remind him of unresolved issues in his own life. Ask other friends, and seek out people in recovery to form the basis of your support.

Setting limits on your own involvements will help you take care of yourself and not get overextended. You may want to make yourself available to others as part of your own recovery, but if you say yes to someone when you'd rather say no, you only end up resenting him. Instead of making up excuses, offer a counterproposal of what you are willing to do, and what you'd like in return. Learning that you can acknowledge another person's needs without having to meet them is an important skill.

Individual Psychotherapy

If friends and support groups do not provide you with as much individual attention as you would like, you may want to explore your issues in greater depth with a licensed psychotherapist.

In some parts of the gay community, people talk openly about being in therapy, but it still carries a stigma for many men. They think that seeing a "shrink" means that you're crazy, so they won't see anyone for help even if they are suffering a great deal of emotional pain. Just as a physician sees people with heart attacks as well as people with broken bones or the flu, psychotherapists also deal with a wide range of client issues. While they treat some people who are very disoriented, they also see people who feel anxious or depressed, who have problems in their relationships, or who are experiencing post-traumatic symptoms. They see people in recovery from substance abuse, compulsive behavior, and dysfunctional families. Therapy can assist people who want support in adjusting to major loss or changes, who feel stuck, or who simply want more access to their feelings. You don't have to be crazy to seek help from psychotherapy.

A therapist can help you gain more access to your emotions and avoid repeating unconscious patterns. In therapy you may reevaluate coping strategies that you developed at an early age to survive, but which may now interfere with career goals, intimate relationships, or other interests. You also examine the values that you absorbed from your family and assess whether they hold you back or support you in your growth and self-esteem. The therapist can help you pace access to your feelings so that you don't feel overwhelmed. At the same time, therapy provides some structure and focus so you can continue your progress.

Psychotherapy is not just an exercise in insight. It helps you to realize that you have choices about how you want to live your life. You learn how to counter the negative messages that you absorbed as a child, how to nurture yourself, and how to make changes in your behavior. By identifying and working through your feelings, you no longer feel so constrained by the circumstances of your past.

If you have been using alcohol and other drugs in an addictive manner, the therapist may require that you enter a recovery program before you go into therapy. The reason for this requirement is that you will have little access to your feelings if you are still using, and you won't learn more productive ways to cope with difficult emotions if you can always escape by getting high.

Choosing a therapist is a process of mutual assessment: The therapist wants to understand what your issues are, and you need to figure out whether you feel comfortable with his or her approach. You can call and speak to a few therapists on the phone before you make an appointment. You may want to schedule interviews with more than one therapist to get a better feel for their styles of therapy. It takes a while to develop trust in a therapeutic relationship, but some initial impressions will help guide you in your choice of a therapist. Does she listen to you and understand what you are trying to say? Does he have some experience with the issues you are dealing with? Do you feel comfortable enough to talk about your true concerns?

Despite the fact that homosexuality has been officially removed from the American Psychiatric Association's list of mental disorders, there are still some therapists who try to treat homosexuality as an illness. It is important to find out whether a therapist is able to help you with the issues you want to work on without trying to "cure" your homosexuality.[1] When you ask about a therapist's approach to gay-related issues, he may want to explore how *you* feel about your sexual orientation. This is a legitimate therapeutic concern, but as a consumer of psychotherapy you also have the right to know what you are being treated for.

Group Therapy

Group therapy can be very healing for survivors of early childhood abuse. Group therapy is similar to self-help groups in that it provides a community of support for working through post-traumatic symptoms. A major difference is that in group therapy a psychotherapist trained in group process guides the group's interactions. This guidance can allow greater depth in your discussion by providing some focus and facilitating feedback among the group's members.

If you've had a difficult time getting in touch with your own feelings, it's often easier to feel anger and sorrow in response to hearing someone else's story. Identifying with their experience may elicit memories and feelings about your own abuse. Understanding what they have gone through also can help you feel less judgmental toward yourself. Over time, you realize that you have a lot in common with the other members of the group. You begin to understand that your reactions made sense and that you weren't to blame for your own abuse. Given your limitations as a child, you did the best you could to survive.

The group provides a safe setting in which you can explore your feelings, get useful feedback, and try out new ways of relating. As you develop trust in the group, you'll feel more confident about your ability to work through your feelings, assert your needs, and negotiate conflicts.

Within the group, you can find a balance of challenging yourself to take some risks, while at the same time making sure that you have the support you need to integrate changes into the rest of your life. Everyone heals at his own pace. Some men will be very excited about a personal breakthrough and will encourage others to try the same thing. You may find a group member's confrontation with his family inspiring, for example, but it's important to judge for yourself what feels right for you. Be wary of charismatic leaders who exhort you to throw off defenses before you are ready, or who put you down for not taking chances. A supportive leader will invite you to share feelings or look at certain patterns in your behavior, but he or she will encourage you to proceed at your own pace.

What to Expect in Group Therapy

The whole concept of group therapy is foreign to a lot of people. Knowing what to expect can help you feel more confident about making a commitment to a group therapy experience. The following description is derived from the therapy groups I have run for men who were sexually, physically, and emotionally abused as children (see acknowledgments). This model isn't the only way to run a group, but it will give you an idea of what you might expect in a group dealing with childhood abuse.[2]

Time Frame

Groups can be time-limited or ongoing. The advantage of joining a time-limited group is that you know in the beginning how many times the group will meet. We don't expect that someone will resolve all of their abuse issues within one or even a few twelve-week cycles, but we have found that many abuse survivors find it easier to make a commitment for a specific length of time. At the end of the cycle, you can evaluate how the group fits in with your overall goals for treatment. People often sign up for the next cycle, or they take a break for a few months and come back later. The advantage of a longer commitment is that more cohesiveness and trust develop in the group. Sometimes a group that has been together for one or two cycles will decide to make a commitment for a longer period of time.

Composition

Some groups for abuse survivors include men who were sexually, physically, and emotionally abused in the same group. My colleagues and I have found that it's useful to have separate groups for sexual abuse survivors. The reason for this is that sexual abuse is often more difficult to acknowledge and talk about, so it may get lost in a more general discussion of childhood abuse. However, there are not always enough male sexual abuse survivors available to form a separate group. If you were sexually abused and a more specialized group is not offered, you may still benefit from a group that deals with general abuse issues.

Men who were abused as children often anticipate feeling uncomfortable in a group of men. The majority were abused by men, and many felt alienated by typical male role expectations while they were growing up. The group is organized with the intent to make it safe to talk about the effects of male socialization and homophobia. Some gay men prefer to be in a group with only gay men, but the men in our mixed groups were also able to provide one another with a great deal of support. Both gay and straight men found that they had much more in common than they thought they would.

Assessment Interview

Before the group begins, you will be invited for an initial interview with the group leader(s). This interview is a mutual assessment of whether this is the best group for you. It gives you an opportunity to ask questions about the therapist's background and expectations for the group. You will discuss the group's goals, how the group will be run, and the ground rules for participation. The therapist needs to assess whether you are at a point where you have access to some memories or feelings about what happened to you, but are not so overwhelmed by feelings that it's difficult for you to function in your daily life.[3]

Even this initial interview can bring up a lot of feelings and memories. It's helpful for you to have discussed the abuse in individual therapy in preparation for entering a group so that you are accustomed to dealing with some of the feelings that are likely to arise. Having group and individual therapy at the same time provides a helpful balance of support: Group creates a safe setting in which you can try out new behavior, and then you can talk with your individual therapist about how you felt in reaction to the feelings and memories stimulated by the group. The group can evoke a lot of strong feelings and memories, so it's important for the group therapist to coordinate treatment with your individual therapist. (Your therapists will need your signed permission to discuss your progress and issues. You can request that they tell you about their discussions, and you also have the right to see your records.)

Not everyone is ready for group when they first get in touch with memories and feelings about early abuse. If you have had recent suicidal thoughts or attempts, or if you are in early recovery from substance abuse, it's best to work on these issues in individual therapy for six months to a year before joining a therapy group. It's also wise to postpone group therapy if you are in crisis over a breakup with a lover, the death of a friend, a job loss, a positive HIV test, or other major changes in your life. If you are already in crisis, the onrush of feelings that can occur in group therapy may be overwhelming. You need to have some practice in dealing with memories and feelings a little at a time in your recovery group and in individual therapy so that you're not tempted to abuse drugs or act self-destructively after group. Even if you are not ready for group therapy, you can still get additional support from twelve-step or other self-help groups.

Ground Rules for Group Therapy

The following ground rules are common for group therapy:

1. Come on time, and come to every session
2. Come to group clean and sober
3. Keep confidentiality
4. Acknowledge socializing

5. No sex between group members
6. Speak for yourself
7. Ask permission before touching another group member

1. Come on time, and come to every session. Consistency and reliability are essential for cohesiveness and trust to develop within the group. If you are sick, you will be expected to call to let your therapist know that you won't be able to make it to group. You may have intense feelings and reactions to the issues that are discussed in group. These feelings are what the group is designed to address. If you stay away, you lose the opportunity to deal with the very issues that brought you to group. You need to be willing to make a commitment to come to group even when you don't feel like it. You can talk about your feelings and reactions and say why you didn't want to come rather than staying away.

If you have a hard time dealing with the feelings and memories elicited by the group, talk to your individual therapist and tell your group therapist. If your ability to cope is overwhelmed for an extended period of time, you and your therapists may decide that it would be better for you to discontinue group for the rest of the current cycle. This doesn't mean that you're a failure. No one can predict beforehand what sort of memories may arise when people begin to explore early abuse. You may need to approach these memories and feelings more gradually in individual therapy before you are ready to deal with them in a group setting.

2. Come to group clean and sober. If you have been abusing alcohol and other drugs, you will be expected not to be using for the duration of the group. Recovery is inhibited by the use of chemicals, so even if you haven't been abusing drugs or alcohol, you may also want to stop using any substances (other than those prescribed by your doctor) during the course of the group. All clients, whether or not they have abused substances in the past, will be expected not to use any mind-altering substances for twenty-four hours before or after group. This rule insures that you will be emotionally present during the group and that you don't escape afterward from the emotions that arise in response to the group.

3. Keep confidentiality. Names of group members are kept confidential. You are welcome to discuss *your own* feelings and reactions to the group with friends, but you agree not to talk about the details of other members' stories outside of the group. Even if you don't mention someone's name, people can often be identified from the specific circumstances of their stories. This agreement enables everyone in the group to feel safer about disclosing very personal issues.

4. Acknowledge socializing. Members are welcome to contact one another for support, but it's up to you whether you want to share telephone numbers or initiate outside contact. This is a little different from self-help groups, in which group members are actively encouraged to make contact outside of group. It's fine to do so if you wish, but it is also fine if you prefer to limit your contact to the group. It's helpful to acknowledge any contacts you have had outside the group with other group members during the check-in period (described below) so that there are no secret connections going on within the group.

5. No sex between group members. It is recommended that you not get involved in a sexual relationship with other group members during the course of the group. If you are interested in pursuing a relationship once the group ends, that's up to you. The reason for this guideline is that sexual contact creates a dual relationship during the course of the group: You are members of a group, and you are also sexually or romantically involved. This dual relationship can interfere with both members' free and open discussion of feelings, since your current partner is also in the group. For the same reason, it's important for men who are already in an intimate relationship (or even a close friendship) to join separate groups.

6. Speak for yourself. You will be encouraged to speak for yourself about your own feelings rather than analyzing the feelings of other group members or having intellectual debates. You may discuss the consequences of homophobia, male socialization, or child abuse, but the therapists will encourage you to bring the discussion back to your own emotional response to these issues.

This is not an encounter group, in which everyone is free to let fly with whatever impulse or impression pops into his mind. The group needs to be safe for everyone's participation. If someone feels angry toward a group member, he will be encouraged to identify what the other person's story reminds him of rather than analyzing or attacking the other person.

7. Ask permission before touching another group member. Because the physical and sexual boundaries of so many abuse survivors have been violated, group therapy needs to be an environment in which these boundaries are clear. Some self-help groups encourage hugging and touching, so therapy groups might seem a little more formal and less spontaneous because of this rule. The advantage, however, is that you can decide for yourself whether you feel comfortable about being touched by another group member. This rule allows members to discover their own comfort level around touch, rather than assuming that they have to touch other people because it's expected of them.

Format for the Group

The format for each group session consists of four main sections:

1. A check-in at the beginning
2. Listening to a member's story or discussion of a topic
3. Reactions and feedback from other members
4. A check-out at the end

1. Check-in. During the check-in, each person has a chance to talk about his feelings since the last session and report on any recent developments. These might include contact with family, codependency issues with friends or lovers, health problems, conflict over whether to confront his abusers, or reactions to the previous week's discussion.

2. Telling your story. After the first two or three meetings, most of the groups are spent listening to one member's story. The therapist may suggest a topic of discussion if no one is ready to tell his story or after everyone has finished. Depending on the structure of the group, you may want to sign up ahead of time, or choose to tell your story spontaneously. We encourage members to discuss their plans with their individual therapists ahead of time. After the member tells his story, the therapists ask him how it felt to talk about what happened to him.

The experience of telling your story to a receptive group of men with similar experiences is usually very powerful, healing, and validating. However, no one is *required* to tell his story. We emphasize that you can change your mind about telling your story at any time, because we want you to feel in complete control over your disclosure. This is in contrast to the coercion you may have felt while being sexually, physically, or emotionally abused as a child.

3. Feedback from other members. Following your story, you have an opportunity to hear reactions from other group members. They take turns identifying parts of your history that touched them emotionally. This process deepens the sense of commonality among members of the group. Telling your story in front of a group is a courageous step to take, and you deserve recognition for doing so. You also get a chance to say what it was like to get this feedback. If you signed up to tell your story and then changed your mind, you also deserve recognition for asserting your need to take care of yourself.

4. Check-out. For smaller groups, you may have enough time for a check-out at the end. Group members say how they felt about the evening and mention what they would like to focus on in their own recovery work. The leader may make some observations about the issues that came up during the group. You may have a number of feelings and reactions in response to the group after you go home. Reach out to other members for support and talk about your reactions in individual therapy. You might want to think of at least one nurturing thing you could do for yourself during the week.

Overview of the Group Sessions

First week: Introductions and discussing the effects of abuse. In the first session, group members introduce themselves with their name and a brief description of what brought them to the group at this time. We then ask the question "How were you affected by the abuse?" The group generates a list of dozens of effects, which we write on the board (the combined list from nine groups is included in Appendix I). We ask group members to take a few moments to read through the list and feel what comes up for them.

Putting this list together generates a lot of feelings. Some men wonder whether they will ever be able to deal with all of these effects. Some feel hurt and very angry that they are still affected by the abuse. Others feel affirmed by the fact that they had many reactions in common with the other men in the group. They know that something *happened* to them; they didn't just imagine it.

As a way of normalizing your experience, we point out that these effects are common symptoms of post-traumatic stress. Through the course of the group, you will see how many of your symptoms result from the abuse you suffered; they are not an inherent part of your personality. For many group members, this insight is a revelation and very liberating, because it offers them hope that they can actually heal from the abuse and make changes in their lives. You may be able to identify some areas in which you have already made some progress.

Making this list also provides a safe and limited context for disclosing some of the effects you have suffered. You have the chance to experience some commonality with other members without going into detail about your stories in the very first session. At the end of the meeting, you can share what it was like to be in a group like this. It's a significant step to come to a group and talk about these issues with other men.

Second week: Goals. During the check-in of the second week, we ask what the previous week was like and what feelings came up afterward. Members often have gotten in touch with a lot of anger in the intervening days. Along with this anger comes a determination not to let the effects of the abuse keep them from moving ahead with their lives. Others may feel discouraged and self-conscious about admitting their discouragement if everyone else seems determined. We emphasize that healing consists of acknowledging *whatever* they feel. No one is expected to put on a happy face or pretend everything is fine when it isn't. Hearing this reassurance that they can be honest about their feelings in the group is often a big relief.

After the check-in, members share their hopes and goals. Naturally, getting over the effects of early abuse is most members' purpose in joining the group. Your therapist can help you identify a modest goal that can be attained in twelve weeks, such as feeling more comfortable when talking about your feelings or making some specific changes in your behavior.

Third week: What happened when you first tried to tell someone about your abuse? During this session, we talk about what sort of response you got when you first tried to tell what happened to you. How did you feel about this response? If you never actually told anyone as a child, can you identify any behavior that a sensitive adult might have noticed as a clue that something was wrong?

We also talk about what it's been like for you to share your experiences as an adult. Some members have received a lot of support, while others encounter disbelief or even blame. They may have friends who try to talk them out of feeling bad about something that happened many years ago, which only reinforces the feeling that there must be something wrong with them. We emphasize the importance of healing at your own pace and that it takes time to sort through the effects of early abuse. At the end of the third week, we remind members that the bulk of the next seven sessions will focus on their stories.

Fourth through tenth weeks: Telling your story. The group provides you with the opportunity to tell your story. You may say whatever you want to share about your family background, the circumstances of your abuse, whether you tried to tell anyone, and any details you feel comfortable sharing. You may want to bring in childhood photos, journal entries, letters, pictures, or poems to help you remember and tell your story. Some men like to bring in a teddy bear or other stuffed animal that gives them some comfort and support.

Cohesiveness and trust develop through the mutual sharing of members' stories. Hearing other men's stories validates your own experience and promotes healing. Telling your story also can help you feel more certain of your memories. Because the other men have suffered similar abuse, they understand what you are going through. You realize that post-traumatic symptoms are a natural response to trauma and that you're not crazy for experiencing these effects. Group members also give you feedback about the skills you have developed in the course of your own survival, and you receive support for making changes in your current life.

At the end of the session, we suggest to the man who told his story that he may experience a lot of feelings during the coming week. He may have new memories, get in touch with sorrow and rage, or begin to doubt whether anything he said was true. He may also feel incredibly relieved, feel believed for the first time, acknowledged for his efforts, and appreciated for his willingness to share his experience. At the next session, we invite him to begin the check-in, which gives him a chance to talk about how he felt during the week. This also provides some continuity between one week and the next.

Eleventh week: Effects on intimacy and sexuality. After everyone who wants to has had a chance to tell his story, we have a session in which we talk about the effects of abuse on intimate and sexual relationships. This brings up many issues that could easily become the focus of another therapy group. By now we are planning our next twelve-week cycle, so we ask the members to let us know if they are interested in continuing.

Twelfth week: Appreciations. In the last session, we plan a feedback exercise in which each man who wants to can become the focus of the group's appreciation. The understanding is that you don't respond or answer during the time that others are giving their comments (except to say ''thank you'' if you wish to say something). The reason for this is that some men have a hard time hearing appreciations without discounting them. We acknowledge that in the past they may have gotten compliments that had an ulterior motive, so it may take a while to trust other people's comments.

The feedback consists of each member saying what he appreciates about you. We don't expect anyone to make things up or to try to flatter you; these comments can be very simple positive attributes that each person has seen in you. They may identify parts of your story or participation in the group that they could relate to, that inspired them, and that they appreciated. Then we check in with you to ask how it feels to receive this feedback. If you are accustomed to putting yourself down, it may be difficult not to discount what you have heard. Because a certain level of cohesiveness and trust has developed within the group, however, most of the men are able to accept at least some of this heartfelt appreciation.

We acknowledge the courage and stamina that it takes to participate in such a group. Members have the opportunity to go around one last time to say what they have gotten out of the group. These shared thoughts often include insight, support, nurturing, and a vision of what it means for them to heal from the abuse they have suffered. They also gain the confidence to continue with this process on their own.

Later sessions. The model outlined above is that of a fairly structured group, designed to facilitate a sense of safety, trust, and cohesiveness. Throughout the cycle, there is a lot of discussion of post-traumatic symptoms, suggestions for working through feelings, countering negative messages, getting support for changing behaviors, and self-nurturing.

Groups of men that continue into a second or third cycle with most of the same members provide an opportunity to focus on a deeper level of recovery work. They often get in touch with more vivid memories and make clearer connections between dysfunctional families and current behavior patterns. As trust and cohesiveness develop, there is more room for direct engagement and feedback among members.

As the membership of the group shifts between twelve-week commitments, new members may join the group. Although it may take a while to reestablish the cohesiveness of the group, everyone can benefit from the entry of new people: Old members affirm and strengthen their own recovery by reaching out to newcomers; new members feel inspired and motivated by the progress that others have already made.

Drama, art, dance, and other expressive arts therapies can also be valuable adjuncts to this work. Some men might want to role-play a confrontation with their perpetrators or reenact a childhood scene the way they wish it had turned out. They might want to express their vision of healing through movement, drawing, or poetry. Members can bring in projects they have worked on during the week to share with the rest of the group. There really is no limit to the creative ways in which the group can be used to further the process of healing.

As you see others improve in their ability to get in touch with feelings and make changes in their lives, the group helps you work through feelings and develop a vision of how you might recover from your own abusive past. Feeling empathy for others allows you to cultivate a loving kindness and compassion toward your own child self.

Relating These Ideas to
Your Own Experience

- How do you feel about reaching out to friends when feelings come up for you?
- How do you feel about others asking you for support?
- What has your own experience been like with individual or group psychotherapy?
- If you've never been in therapy, under what circumstances could you see yourself using therapy in the future?

12

▼

Self-Empowerment

As gay men, we continue to be confronted with homophobic attitudes and the threat of assault in our daily lives. We need to find ways to maintain our sense of mutual support in the face of family rejection, public harassment, and social discrimination. In this final chapter, we will look at countering codependency and setting limits in current relationships; the option of confrontation and the issue of forgiveness in abusive families; and how to mobilize ourselves for positive change in a homophobic society.

Countering Codependency

Codependency is a strategy for coping with an unreliable partner when you're unable or unwilling to set appropriate limits. The source of this strategy can often be traced to adaptive responses within a dysfunctional family system. The early message "You are not okay" forms the basis for codependent behavior. As a young child, you may have tried to anticipate others' needs, which at least allowed you to feel some worth by taking care of others. You may still be trying to provide the nurturing for others that you lacked as a child. Without a clear notion from your family about what to expect in a nurturing relationship, you may give in to others' demands or put up with unreliable behavior.

In this section, we will look at how to establish your own sense of boundaries and personal rights. We will also provide some suggestions for countering the negative messages that may emerge when you set limits with your partner or members of your family.

Boundaries

Boundaries are self-identified limits and rights that establish your own sense of personal integrity. In an intimate relationship, you will naturally want to be sensitive to your partner's desires, yet it may be difficult to assess your own needs if you grew up in a chaotic or intrusive family. You may feel confused about what to expect in relationships at work, with friends, or with an intimate partner. You may put up with inappropriate behavior because you don't realize that you have the right to your own thoughts, feelings, and privacy. Listed below are the personal rights that everyone should be able to insist upon in their family, friendships, and intimate relationships.

Personal Rights

- The right to have your own thoughts
- The right to make your own decisions
- The right to have your own feelings
- The right to privacy
- The right to control your own property
- The right to exert control over your own body

Let's go through this list to see how you can put these personal rights into practice in your own relationships.

The right to have your own thoughts. Dysfunctional families have poor communication skills. They may lash out rather than trying to understand each other, or attempt to read your mind and tell you what you are "really" thinking. Many people feel brainwashed by their families. They grow up believing that they are stupid, that they will never amount to anything, and that what they think is unimportant. You have the right to think whatever you want and take in new information when it makes sense to you.

The right to make your own decisions. You may have been told what to do with little consideration for what you wanted for yourself. You may be curious about others' experience or look to others for guidance, but it's up to you to make decisions about how you want to earn a living, where you want to live, and with whom you want to be friends.

The right to have your own feelings. Children in dysfunctional families are constantly told how to feel. Sadness is ridiculed and anger is considered a hostile attack that must be subdued. Even positive feelings may be cautioned against, lest they give rise to "unreasonable" expectations. You have the right to feel however you feel. Even if your feelings don't make much sense in the moment, there are probably good reasons for feeling the way you do. As you gain more access to your feelings, you can figure out how you want to respond to them.

The right to privacy. You have the right to privacy in your own living space. You also have the right to privacy in letters, phone calls, and conversations. You can choose whether to share your thoughts and feelings or keep them to yourself. You also have the right to expect that others will take the time to listen to you and understand you if they want a relationship with you.

The right to control your property. You may not have had anything that you could call your own. Family members may have taken your money or used your property without permission. You can decide whether to share your possessions, lend people money, or let people stay with you.

The right to exert control over your own body. Abused children rarely have the sense that they have control over their own bodies. They are forced to fetch and serve, they are hit at whim, and they are used sexually. If they protest, they are punished. *You have the right to your own body.* You can determine who may touch you, how you want to be touched, and when.

As you become closer to your partner, you will naturally want to share more of yourself and find out more about him. You begin to take his thoughts and feelings into consideration as well as your own, especially when they have an impact on sharing a life together. However, you don't have to give up any of your personal rights when you enter a relationship. You still have the right to your own thoughts and feelings, even if you are willing to negotiate decisions that affect your life together. You still have the right to make decisions about your own property, even if you want to merge your financial resources. You still have the right to decide how you want to be touched, even if you and your partner have a monogamous relationship.

Setting Limits

What's the difference between setting limits and trying to control someone else's behavior? While it's true that you can't control anyone else, *you don't have to let anyone abuse you.* Setting a limit with another adult is a way to clarify your unwillingness to participate in abusive or codependent behavior. For example, if your partner wants you to call in sick for him at work because he's hung over, you can decline to do so. If he violates any of your personal rights, you can object. If he isn't willing to negotiate with you during disagreements, or if he consistently refuses to take your feelings and needs into consideration, you can insist that you both get couples counseling. If he threatens you or tries to harm you, you can call the police and get whatever help you need to sever your relationship. Although you can't control other people, you can set limits on abusive and unreliable behavior. Once you feel good enough about yourself to set appropriate limits, you are well on your way to recovery from codependency.

Even though others may have legitimate needs, you don't necessarily have to meet them. You can acknowledge their desires and still maintain your own limits. Don't get into an argument about whether you're self-centered or whether their needs are legitimate. You don't have to justify yourself, nor do you need to gain their approval. Asserting your needs doesn't mean that you can't negotiate, but remember that negotiations take *both* individuals' needs into consideration. You can acknowledge another person's needs and let him know whether or not you are available to meet them.

The need for support in recovery from codependency is as great as it is in other kinds of recovery. This support is available through individual and group therapy, as well as through family-related twelve-step programs such as Al-Anon, Adult Children of Alcoholics, and Codependents Anonymous. These groups will help you understand the dynamics in your family that led to your own pattern of coping. It's often easier to understand other people's situations before you reach clarity about patterns in your own relationships. You can see that others have the right to expect reliable behavior from their families and partners, and you gradually begin to claim this right for yourself. As you feel more comfortable with setting limits to unacceptable behavior, you can get out of uncomfortable situations and stop the cycle of revictimization. You no longer see your own happiness as being dependent on your ability to control someone else, and you gain confidence in determining the course of your own life.

Couples in Recovery

It's common in alcohol and substance abuse recovery programs to hear the suggestion that you spend a solid year in recovery before you pursue a romantic relationship. It is difficult enough to sort through your own feelings in early recovery without being thrust into a relationship with another man who has all his own needs and issues to deal with.

If you are already in a relationship when you enter recovery, you may notice some changes in your interactions. As you get more in touch with feelings and memories from your own family, you may identify dysfunctional patterns in your current relationship. These patterns often become more obvious when one partner begins to change. When you alter the equilibrium of a codependent relationship, the other partner is likely to react by trying to restore the previous balance. If you discover unspoken assumptions about what role each of you is expected to play in your relationship, you may want to renegotiate some of these expectations.

It's easy to take each other's moods and feelings personally in early recovery. If your partner is upset, you can listen to his feelings and try to understand his problem without having to solve it for him. Similarly, if you are upset with your partner, you can say how you feel, tell him what issues his behavior has brought up for you, and give him a chance to say how he feels, too. If you feel insecure about your partner's interest in other men, for example, you can talk about how you feel without demanding that he stop seeing his friends. Use your feelings instead as a clue to previous times when you felt left out or abandoned. This will help you grieve for the earlier loss, and you'll gain a clearer idea about what you want from your current relationship. You may need to set practical limits about what you are willing to put up with, but don't leap to threats or ultimatums simply to demonstrate that you are hurt. Try to understand each other's feelings and negotiate a mutually satisfactory solution.

Some couples are not able to adjust to these changes, especially if only one partner is in recovery. If both of you are committed to working through the issues that arise, you may be able to reach a new equilibrium that meets the needs of both partners. However, both of you will need support during this period of readjustment. Couples counseling can help you work through emerging feelings without taking your frustrations out on each other.

Confrontation

Realizing that you did not cause your parents to be abusive to you is a significant step in ending the cycle of self-blame and shame that often results in self-defeating behavior. For gay men who grew up in abusive families, this realization can be very healing. This understanding is not just an intellectual insight about child development and dysfunctional families. It is an *emotional realization* that they were innocent children who were treated badly. Although they may experience post-traumatic symptoms, there is nothing inherently wrong with them. They can heal from the trauma of childhood abuse.

Some abuse survivors want to confront their families with their newfound insight. This can be an important step for some people, but it's not for everyone. What is most important is to come to terms with the effects of the abuse on your own life. Then you can decide whether you want to disclose your understanding and current feelings to your family or others who abused you. It's up to you to assess what you hope to gain and weigh the advantages against the liabilities of a direct confrontation. Listed below are some of these advantages and liabilities.

Positive Aspects of Confronting Your Family

- You can express your feelings directly instead of becoming depressed, engaging in self-destructive behavior, or hating yourself.
- You can claim power in your relationship with your family by asserting your personal rights rather than feeling victimized.
- A confrontation may shift the dynamics within your family so that perpetrators can no longer operate in secrecy.
- By speaking up, you may help other family members break through their denial about their abuse and your family's dysfunction.
- Saying what happened to you may help you overcome your fear of being annihilated for disclosing your feelings or for opposing your parents.

Liabilities of Confrontation

- Thinking that you *must* confront your family can reinforce your belief that you need their recognition to heal.

- You may be blamed for having been abused.
- You may risk estrangement from your family if they refuse to deal with your feelings or cut off contact.
- Your family's denial or minimization may reinforce your own self-doubt and self-blame.
- You may risk the danger of being abused again.

It's helpful to think about what you hope to achieve through a confrontation with your perpetrators. Some people simply want to break the conspiracy of silence. Others may confront their families in the hope that their parents will be transformed into the loving and nurturing mother and father they had always longed for. A few parents and siblings are able to acknowledge their mistakes and are willing to work hard to make a new beginning. Most dysfunctional families, however, are not able to deal with feelings very well, which is a large part of why they are dysfunctional. They may refuse to face your feelings or admit their responsibility for your abuse. Some survivors are crushed by the bald-faced denial and blame that they receive in response to their disclosure. Still, for some people it is important to make this attempt. In the face of a hostile rejection, they may realize that it's not healthy for them to continue contact with their family. This can lead to a deeper level of grief as they recognize that their parents may never be able to nurture them.

Confrontation is not a hurdle that everyone has to jump in order to heal from past abuse. For some people it can be a significant step, but each person's situation is unique. The decision to confront your abusers is yours alone. Through group support and individual therapy, you can try to assess whether a direct confrontation is a step that you want to take, weighing the potential benefits against the risk of estrangement from your family. Some people already feel estranged from their abusive families, so they don't feel that they are risking a lot. Others make all the preparations to confront and then change their minds because they have already worked through much of what they had hoped to accomplish in a confrontation. Whatever you decide, make sure that you are doing it for yourself, not to please your therapist or your support group.

Confrontation is not an all-or-nothing experience. You can separate confrontation into three steps and then decide which of these steps would best support your own path of recovery from early abuse.

1. Confronting yourself. The first confrontation is with yourself—you try to assess whether you really were abused. Because of possible repression of memories and denial, it can take a while for you to figure out what happened to you. One day, your memories will seem vivid and clear; the next day you may be filled with doubt. Don't blame yourself for having vague memories or doubts. It takes time to accept that the people who were supposed to look after you may have abused you. It may also be difficult to believe that you didn't deserve whatever abuse you suffered. When you were a child, you may have needed limits set on certain behaviors, but *you did not deserve to be abused.*

2. Setting limits on current behavior. Whether or not you decide to discuss the past with your family, you may want to set limits on their homophobic remarks or their violations of your personal rights. This can be difficult if you're the only one in your family who objects to intrusive or abusive behavior. When you start asserting your own needs, you may get a negative reaction from your family for violating your usual role. They may accuse you of being selfish and uncooperative, which reinforces your own insecurity about going against their injunctions. You may get in touch with internalized messages that echo your family's accusations and undermine your desire to take care of yourself. Listed below are some of the underlying beliefs that may emerge when you assert your needs or set limits on abusive or unreliable behavior:

Negative Messages: You are basically a selfish person, so you can't trust your own needs. Your needs aren't important. Your worth is dependent on deferring to others. No one could ever love you for yourself. If you assert yourself, it will only prove how selfish you really are. Everyone will know that you were the cause of your family's problems.

You can counter each of these beliefs with more realistic statements of your true abilities:

- You are basically a selfish person, so you can't trust your own needs.
▶ I *can* trust my own needs and negotiate with others when our needs are in conflict.

- Your needs aren't important.
▶ My needs are just as important as anyone else's.

- Your worth is dependent on deferring to others.
▶ I can take care of myself and still cooperate with others.

- No one could ever love you for yourself.
▶ I am lovable just the way I am. I don't have to defer to others to gain their love.

- If you assert yourself, it will only prove how selfish you really are.
▶ I can assert my needs and still take other people's needs into consideration.

- Everyone will know that you were the cause of your family's problems.
▶ Our problems arose because we weren't getting our needs met. We can recognize that we all deserve nurturing, love, empathy, and acceptance. By asserting my own rights, I'm not trying to take them away from anyone else.

3. Disclosure of past resentments. The third level is a frank disclosure of past resentments toward family members who abused you. A confrontation does not have to be abusive, hostile, or threatening. A confrontation can be a simple statement that consists of four elements:

1. What your abusers did to you
2. How it affected you
3. How you feel about it now
4. How you want to be treated in your current relationship

If you decide to confront your abusers, get support from others who have gone through a similar experience so that you will be prepared to deal with the upheaval, accusations, and other fallout that may follow your disclosure. Your therapist and support group members can help you examine the hopes and fears you have about potential responses. They can also help you plan a confrontation that ensures your own safety. You can write a letter, meet in a public place, or have a family therapist facilitate your meeting. If your abusers are not available, or if you have no desire to deal with them face-to-face, you can still say what you want to say—to an empty chair, in your journal, or in an unsent letter. Practicing what you want to say is good preparation if you decide that you want to confront them directly.

When confronted with their abusive behavior, your perpetrators may respond with denial, minimization, or blame. They may deny that anything occurred and try to distort your memories. They may say that it happened such a long time ago that you shouldn't dwell on the past. When accused of sexual abuse, perpetrators may claim that you imagined the whole thing or that *you* seduced *them*. They may try to convince other relatives that your accusation is proof of how unstable you are. A refusal by your perpetrators to accept responsibility can be infuriating, but you can't control whether other people will admit how they abused you. Insisting on an acknowledgment of their abusive behavior can lead to self-blame and a sense of failure. By demanding an act of contrition that you're not likely to get, you continue to give them power over you.

When you have worked through a lot of your own feelings about the abuse, *your perception of what happened no longer depends on your perpetrator's ability to own up to it.* You may simply want to tell him (or her) that you know what he did to you and explain how it affected you. The confrontation is for your own recovery, not for his. You can anticipate what he might say and practice responses that keep you focused and in control of the session, but you don't need to measure your success by whether or not he can admit his guilt. *The confrontation was successful if you said what you had to say.* If he owns up to his abuse and feels motivated to work on his own issues concerning inappropriate and violent behavior, that's up to him.

Regardless of whether or not he admits any responsibility, you may want to make concrete demands for specific changes if you are to have contact in the future. These might include alcoholism treatment, domestic violence counseling, or family therapy. If you have children, you might want to insist that another adult be present when he sees them. If he refuses, you may need to decide if you want any contact with him at all.

You may feel torn because your relatives meet for holidays, and it's difficult to have contact with those family members whom you trust without seeing your perpetrator. You may choose to make other arrangements to see some of your relatives, or you may see the family together and simply keep interaction with your abuser to a minimum. All of these suggestions for confrontation or setting limits depend on what you want in your own recovery. *You do not have to confront or have contact with your abusers to heal from previous trauma.*

Confrontations and Coming Out

For gay men, early abuse may be mixed together with rejection, ridicule, and harassment for being gay or for not conforming to masculine stereotypes. Gay men from dysfunctional families may be further abused when they come out. If you decide that you want to come out as well as confront your family over previous abuse, you may want to come out first and see how they react, or you may want to deal with resentments over past abuse and then decide whether you still want to come out.

Coming out to a dysfunctional family *and* disclosing resentments over past abuse can be a very complicated process, with a high risk for escalation of conflict and repeated abuse. *You don't have to come out to your family if they are likely to abuse you.* It's up to you to decide whether coming out or a confrontation over past abuse is in your own best interests. You may want to write a letter to gauge their initial reaction. If you decide to pursue this disclosure in person, it might be useful to hire a family therapist to mediate your confrontation and your coming out process over a number of sessions. Your therapist can make it clear to your family that there will be no violence or threats of violence during or between sessions. If your family is not able to abide by this rule, you would be wise to end contact with them and obtain a restraining order if they continue to threaten you.

Some of the above examples include worst-case scenarios. Not every dysfunctional family continues to be abusive once the children have grown up. However, the families of many gay men make it clear that they prefer not to talk about their son's homosexuality. You may have a partner, gay friends, and gay-related involvements through work, recreation, politics, or church, so there may not be much left to talk about besides the weather if you can't refer to homosexuality. You can open up this discussion by acknowledging that this topic is something they have preferred to avoid, but that you would like to be able to acknowledge more of your life at family gatherings. You can listen to your parents and empathize with their point of view, but you don't have to agree with them. Not agreeing doesn't necessarily mean that you can't have a relationship with them. You can negotiate ways to take their feelings into consideration while still maintaining your self-respect as an openly gay man.

The Issue of Forgiveness

Some men wish they could let go of past hurt and anger and move on with their lives. They believe that if they could just forgive and forget, they wouldn't have to feel the hurt, anger, and sadness. However, a premature leap toward forgiveness may suppress your feelings. If you haven't worked through the underlying pain, you may become depressed instead. You are more likely to feel some compassion for the limitations of your abusers *after* you have allowed yourself to feel the hurt and anger for how you were treated.

An overemphasis on the importance of forgiveness fosters unnecessary guilt. For survivors of severe childhood abuse or for adult survivors of trauma such as assault, torture, or rape, *forgiveness may never feel appropriate*. Not forgiving doesn't mean that you will inhibit your own healing. It just means that you are keeping up your guard to protect yourself from further injury, especially by those who refuse to admit their part in harming you.

It's common to feel ambivalent about your parents. If your middle-aged or elderly parents no longer seem like such tyrannical monsters, it may be difficult to validate your memories of early abuse. Even with abusive family members, you may have had some moments that felt comfortable or nurturing. You may appreciate some of the ways that your practical needs were provided for, even if you wish that you had received more attention for your feelings. You may resent the abuse you endured even if you also appreciate the fact that your parents suffered from their own hardships. Child abusers were often trauma-tized themselves as children, but never worked through their early abuse. Instead they took out their anger and hurt on you. This is no excuse for their behavior; understanding why it happened doesn't mean that you should condone it. You are taking steps to make sure that you don't continue the cycle of abuse, and you have every right to wish that your own abusers had done the same.

After you have worked through your hurt and anger, you may feel some compassion for the closed and constricted lives of those who abused you, even if they deny any responsibility. Their denial is a reflection of their emotional limitations and has nothing to do with your own self-worth. You don't have to convince them of anything to heal yourself. Knowing that your own recovery doesn't depend on their acknowledgment may allow you to set limits without getting hooked into their denial, minimization, and blame. You can let go of trying to change them and move on with your own life.

Forgiving Yourself

Whether or not you forgive those who abused you, it is vital to rec-ognize how vulnerable you were as a child and to learn how to feel some compassion for your own child self. You can forgive yourself for not having been the impossibly perfect child (or adult) that could have soothed and healed your parents. You can forgive yourself for the fact that you weren't able to prevent the abuse. You can forgive yourself for whatever self-destructive behavior you may have engaged in before you embarked on the road to recovery, and you can forgive yourself when you have setbacks even now.

The more forgiving you are toward yourself, the better you will feel and the less likely you are to engage in self-destructive behavior. You also will develop more realistic expectations about the pace of your own growth. As you develop your capacity for self-forgiveness, you can provide yourself with the nurturing, love, and acceptance that you may never have received from your family.

Combating Homophobia

Understanding the sources of internalized oppression can allow us to work through feelings so that we no longer blame ourselves. Instead of punishing ourselves with self-defeating behavior, we can reach out for support. Gay people have a unique opportunity to form coalitions with progressive men and women, the disabled, and ethnic minorities because we are included in all of these groups. We can reach out to civil rights and religious groups by emphasizing the values and goals we have in common. We can join together in education and consciousness-raising that combat interpersonal prejudice and institutionalized sexism, racism, and homophobia.

To build these coalitions, we need to challenge the misconceptions and prejudices that divide us. When prejudice stems largely from ignorance, interaction with people from another group may counter preconceptions, but not just any experience will do. Superficial encounters may even serve to maintain and reinforce negative beliefs. Listed below are the qualities of contact that tend to lessen tension and prejudice between groups of people who perceive one another as being different.[1]

1. Intimate, ongoing interactions. A work situation or a friendship may provide corrective experiences for the person who isn't aware of previous contacts with gay people. Getting to know and like someone and then finding out he is gay will often cause a shift in attitudes of people whose misconceptions are largely based on ignorance and lack of contact.

2. Experience of shared beliefs around other values. Recognizing that people have similar beliefs about other values can diminish the sense of threat from superficial differences. These might be common religious or political beliefs, or simply the belief that other people should be treated with respect. Common interests can also help to overcome prejudice by emphasizing similarities. Once we perceive our common humanity, we are less likely to feel threatened by cultural differences.

3. Cooperation toward similar goals. A task that requires working together can break down prejudice within the group. Cooperating with people from different backgrounds at work, at church, on a committee, in athletics, or as a neighbor toward a common goal can develop trust, cohesiveness, and mutual identification as members of the same team. All of these contacts can be developed in our schools, churches, and at work to break down stereotypes and build a coalition for the civil and human rights of all our citizens.

Whenever a minority group takes a stand, whether through politics or direct action, it may elicit some backlash that further ignites the group's passion. We can expect a certain amount of self-righteousness in any movement for liberation, as centuries of oppression are unlocked and whole lifetimes of anguish are released. Some men become savvy politicians who can work within the system. Some need to ventilate their anger over personal hurt and current injustice. Others enjoy celebrating the diversity and creativity of our lifestyles, even if some of the people we are trying to influence might be offended.

We may not always agree on tactics, but we can try to listen to one another and understand our differences rather than immediately assuming that anyone who disagrees with us is our enemy. There is room for many different kinds of approaches, from the development of legal strategies to the impassioned speech or from the calm description of scientific knowledge to noisy demonstrations and civil disobedience. Each of us can find a way to combat homophobia and heterosexism that fits our own personality, style, and talents.

Creating Your Own Life

Through this book, I hope to provide a glimpse of the quality of life that is possible for gay men who have worked through the trauma of growing up in a dysfunctional family within a homophobic culture. We shouldn't blame ourselves for the guilt and shame we experienced when we became aware of our attraction toward other males. We can accept the fact that we have been injured by this trauma, as well as recognize that we can heal from these wounds. Survivors of dysfunctional and homophobic families develop many strengths to cope with their abuse. If your needs for nurturing, love, and acceptance were not met by your parents, you can begin to meet them yourself. You can learn how to cope with self-destructive behavior and other posttraumatic symptoms and reach out to other gay men to form a community of mutual support. As you heal from past abuse, you gain more access to your true talents and abilities.

The gay liberation movement that has grown over the last twenty years has enabled many of us to provide our own self-validation. We may wish that we also had the support of our families and the surrounding culture, but we no longer have to have it to feel good about ourselves. Nonetheless, external homophobia is a relentless source of trauma. Young gay people still grow up in an atmosphere of ignorance and intolerance, isolated from other gays. Despite the insights we have about the process of internalized oppression, it can be very difficult even for gay adults to fend off a constant barrage of threats to our civil liberties, our health, and our right to live without fear of assault.

How can we continue to experience homophobia without internalizing negative messages? We can't change what has happened to us in the past, but as adults we can heal from early abuse and homophobic assaults. By getting support to work through our feelings, we are less likely to internalize shame or engage in self-defeating behavior. We can transform our trauma by re-creating the world as we wish it had been. By confronting discrimination, we can make real changes in the world around us. By participating in others' healing, we heal ourselves. We can feel whatever we feel without guilt or shame and then decide exactly what we want to do with our lives. As we learn how to nurture ourselves and one another, we expand our capacity for meaningful work, physical development, creative interests, and intimate relationships. Together we can form a supportive culture in which we are free to create our own lives and grow according to our true nature.

Appendix I:
Effects of
Childhood Abuse

▼

I compiled the following list from nine therapy groups for men who were sexually, physically, and emotionally abused as children.* Each group included five to seven men who gave their responses to the question "How have you been affected by the abuse you experienced as a child?"†

No one experienced *all* of these effects, and you may have some effects from early abuse that are not listed here. Having any of these effects does not necessarily mean that you were abused as a child; however, it has been useful for the men in our groups to see the range of possible effects from early trauma. Realizing that post-traumatic effects are common reactions to childhood abuse helped them gain some perspective on their symptoms. Rather than blaming themselves for being "messed up," they could see quite clearly that any child who has been traumatized is likely to be severely affected by the abuse.

During the course of the group, we also spend a lot of time highlighting the members' strengths and survival skills. Although some reactions to abuse can result in difficulties as an adult, it's important to remember that many of these reactions are creative strategies for surviving a severely abusive family. For example, it makes a lot of sense for an abused child to shut down emotionally, dissociate, mistrust other people, deny the abuse, or adapt to others' needs. When looking through this list, consider your strengths in the face of the abuse you suffered. Give your own child self credit for surviving the best he knew how.

* For a description of this group, see chapter 11.

† Reading through this list may elicit a lot of feelings and memories. If you are in early recovery from alcohol or substance abuse, or if you have never sought counseling or other support for childhood abuse, please read the Note of Caution in the Introduction before looking over this list.

Besides listing the effects outlined below, the men in these groups were also able to recognize their increasing ability to accept their feelings, develop new choices, and acknowledge their courage. Being in a group with other men helped them to end their isolation and feel some confidence in their ability to heal from trauma and move on with their lives.

I sorted the men's responses into the following categories:

Reactions as a child

Self-image

Effects on relationships:

    Codependency and bound-ary issues

    Effects on intimacy

    Effects on sexuality

    Dealing with others

Depression

Feelings

Dissociation

Self-destructive tendencies

Difficulties with work

Family issues

Health

Other reactions

Reactions as a Child

Belief that no one is any good

Blackmail by abuser

Embarrassment

Fear of being set up

Feeling different

Feeling trapped

Guilt

Helplessness

Insecurity

Keeping a secret

Lack of coping skills

Lack of fun

Loss of control

Not feeling safe

Shame

Surprise

Trouble breathing

Unsafe

Who would believe me?

Self-Image

Inferiority

Internalized ''evil''

Low self-esteem

Poor body image

Self-abuse	Self-reliance
Self-doubt	Undeserving
Self-hatred	Wondering if normal

Effects on Relationships

Codependency and boundary issues:

Adult-child-of-alcoholic issues	Need for validation
Apologetic	Need to separate responsibility for others' reactions
Confusion about physical and emotional boundaries	
	Neediness
Confusion over responsibility	Passive-aggressive
Feeling selfish	People-pleasing
Giving in	Taking care of others
Indifferent to self/helpful to others	Wanting to make self happy, not others
Lack of boundaries	Withdrawal

Effects on intimacy:

Avoidance	Inability to believe anyone could love me
Closed off from others	
Cold	Introverted
Confusion about love	Isolation
Denial of a desire for intimacy	Judgmental of self and others
	Keeping people at a distance
Fear of abandonment	Lack of love
Fear of intimate relationships	Lack of support
Fear of men/women	Loneliness
Having to be in control	Mistrust
Hiding out	Problems with friendships
	Relationship difficulties

Effects on sexuality:

Confusion about sexual orientation

Confusion between sex and love

Confusion over sexuality

Delayed adolescence

Excessive masturbation

Impotence

Injurious sado-masochism

Pornography

Problems with sexual dysfunction

Sensitive to touch

Sexual compulsion/frenzy

Sexual dysfunction

Sexual identity confusion

Sexual/relationship confusion

Dealing with others:

Belief that others won't listen or understand

Control issues

Dealing with other people's ignorance about the abuse

Difficulty being honest with self or others

Embarrassment

Fear of children

Fear of fathering

Fear of men

Fear of response from others

Fear of strangers

Fear of women

Hard to accept compliments

Hard to listen to others without feeling back in abuse

Inability to give and accept

Inability to make friends

Mistrust

Never fitting in

Projecting

Shutting down

Testing

Trouble believing people's good intentions

Ungrateful

Depression

All-or-nothing thinking

Apathy

Assumption of negative

Cynicism

Depression

Despair

Fear of risk

Guilt

Hopelessness

Impending doom

Lack of pleasure

Loneliness

Loss of energy

Negative expectations

Pessimism

Feelings

Discounting myself and my feelings

Emotional control—too much or too little

Emotional pain

Exhaustion

Grief over loss of childhood

Hatred/mistrust of men

Hatred of one's own maleness

Hurt

Misplaced feelings

Moodiness

My feelings don't matter to anyone (or to me)

Not dealing with emotions

Out of balance

Overwhelmed

Overwhelming grief, loss

Panic

Rage

Sadness

Suppression of feelings

Tension

Trouble discussing feelings without getting angry

Trouble keeping little boy inside happy

Trying to get away from feelings

Unexplained feelings

Unfeeling

Worry

Dissociation

Alienation

Detachment

Disconnected

Fantasizing

Feeling split with myself

I don't have a body

Lack of identity

Lack of self

Multiple personality

Never feeling grounded

Spaciness

Time frozen

Self-Destructive Tendencies

Acting out

Addiction to alcohol and other drugs

Bulimia

Compulsive behavior

Eating disorders

Emotional self-abuse

Fear of my own abusiveness

Hiding from what I need to deal with

Irresponsibility

Masochism

Physical self-abuse

Risk-taking—too much or too little—in relationships, work, moves

Sabotage

Sadism

Self-deprivation

Self-mutilation

Suicidal thoughts/feelings

Difficulties with Work

Fear of authority

Fear of success/failure

Indecision

Instability

Issues with authority figures

Lack of confidence

Lack of professional goals

Money problems

Perfectionism

Power

Procrastination

Take on too much

Trouble with limits

Ultraresponsible

Family Issues

Conflict over confrontation

Confusion over how to relate to family of origin

Dealing with parents

Letting go of nonacceptance

Searching for parent in other relationships

Health

Conversion of emotional pain into physical symptoms

Hypochondria

Neglect

Pain

Physical problems

Sleep disturbance

Sometimes I don't know how to care for myself

Other Reactions

Denial of the abuse

Deprived

Difficulty trusting own intuition

Disbelief in memories

Doubting right to be happy

Feeling cheated out of my life

Feeling dysfunctional

Feeling robbed

Hypervigilant

If only

Intrusive dreams and nightmares

Irrational obsessing

Lack of spontaneity

Not knowing what's normal in human growth

Regrets

Resentment over needing recovery groups

Spiritual damage

Surprise over realizing what has happened

Therapy junkie

Why me?

Appendix II:
Resources

▼

Psychotherapy with a licensed therapist is covered by some private health insurance. Licensed therapists include psychologists, social workers, marriage and family counselors, clinical nurse specialists, and psychiatrists. Community-based counseling centers usually have a sliding fee scale. In addition to the directory mentioned under Gay Resources, some gay and gay-sensitive therapists are listed in the advertising sections of gay newspapers. You can also ask friends or other support group members for referrals.

Alcohol and Substance Abuse Resources

Alcoholics Anonymous and other twelve-step programs: Narcotics, Debtors, Overeaters, Gamblers, Sex and Love Addicts, Codependents, Al-Anon, Adult Children of Alcoholics, among others. You can obtain schedules and information about other twelve-step groups by looking up Alcoholics Anonymous in your local telephone directory.

See Barbara Yoder, *Recovery Resources* (New York: Fireside/Simon & Schuster, 1990) for listings. You can also call the National Institute of Drug Abuse Hotline for referrals to treatment centers and local twelve-step groups at (800) 662-HELP.

National Clearinghouse for Alcohol and Drug Information
(800) 729-6686

Secular Organizations for Sobriety
Offers referrals to SOS groups, a secular alternative to twelve-step
    programs.
P.O Box 15781
North Hollywood, CA 91695
(818) 580-8851

Child Abuse

Adult Children of Sexual Dysfunction
P.O. Box 8084
Lake St. Station
110 E. 31st St.
Minneapolis, MN 55408
(include SASE)

National Committee for the Prevention of Child Abuse
Resource clearinghouse.
332 S. Michigan Ave., Suite 1250
Chicago, IL 60614
(312) 663-3520

Survivors of Childhood Abuse Program
Advocacy, education, referrals.
P.O. Box 630
Hollywood, CA 90028
(Call through the Child Help National Child Abuse Hotline: (800)
    422-4453.)

Domestic Violence

Community United Against Violence
Provides groups for gay men who have been battered.
514 Castro St.
San Francisco, CA 94114
(415) 864-3112

Men Overcoming Violence (MOVE)
Provides groups for gay men who batter.
3004-16th St.
San Francisco, CA 94114
(415) 626-6683

The New York City Gay and Lesbian Anti-Violence Project, Inc.
208 W. 13th St.
New York, NY 10011
(212) 807-0197

For domestic violence services in other parts of the country, see Gay Resources, or call:

National Domestic Violence Hotline
(800) 333-7233

Gay Resources

National Gay/Lesbian Health Directory—Sourcebook on Lesbian/Gay Health Care
Published by the National Lesbian and Gay Health Foundation, this directory provides listings of gay providers across the country, from AIDS-related services and health care to substance abuse recovery, psychotherapy, and groups for incest, sexual compulsion, and domestic violence.

National Lesbian and Gay Health Foundation
1638 R St.
Suite 2
Washington, DC 20009
Or P.O. Box 65472
Washington, DC 20035
(202) 797-3708

Multiple Personality

Many Voices
Newsletter for multiple personalities.
P.O. Box 2639
Cincinnati, OH 45201-2636

Ritual Abuse Survivors

Believe in Children
Information and education for parents and child victims of ritual abuse.
P.O. Box 1358
Manhattan Beach, CA 90266

Child Help, USA
Offers referrals to therapists in your area who have experience
    working with ritual abuse.
(800) A CHILD

Report of the Ritual Abuse Task Force
Los Angeles Commission on the Status of Women
383 Hall of Administration
500 W. Temple
Los Angeles, CA 90012
(213) 974-1455

Self-Help

California Self-Help Center
Links with many types of ongoing support groups.
2349 Franz Hall
405 Hildegard Ave.
Los Angeles, CA 90024
Statewide toll-free number: (800) 222-LINK

National Self-Help Clearinghouse
Provides referrals around the country.
City University of New York
33 W. 42nd St. #12222
New York, NY 10036
(212) 840-1259

**The Self-Help Sourcebook: Finding and Forming Mutual Aid
    Self-Help Groups,** E. Madera and A. Meese, eds.
Self-Help Clearinghouse
Saint Clares-Riverside Medical Center
Denville, NJ 07834

Sexual Abuse Support and Referrals

Incest Survivors Anonymous
Twelve-step model self-help groups.
P.O. Box 5613
Long Beach, CA 90805
(213) 428-5599

PLEA— Prevention, Leadership, Education and Assistance
Network of male incest survivors, publishes a quarterly newsletter.
Hank Astrada
Box 22
Zia Road
Santa Fe, NM 87505
(505) 982-9184

Survivors of Incest Anonymous
Clearinghouse for local incest self-help group referrals following the
    twelve-step model of Alcoholics Anonymous.
P.O. Box 21817
Baltimore, MD 21222
Twenty-four-hour line: (301) 282-3400

Voices in Action—Victims of Incest Can Emerge Survivors
National referral network for various special-interest groups dealing
    with specific aspects of incest-related recovery, such as
    dissociation, abuse by authorities of religious communities, abuse
    by mothers, substance abuse, compulsive sexuality, ritual abuse,
    and others. They also offer a "survival packet" for male
    survivors and publish a newsletter.
P.O. Box 148309
Chicago, IL 60614
(312) 327-1500

Notes and References

▼

1: Growing Up Gay in a Homophobic Culture

1. George Weinberg introduced the term homophobia in *Society and the Healthy Homosexual* (New York: St. Martin's Press, 1972).

For an overview of various studies on homophobia, see Stephen Morin and Ellen Garfinkle, "Male Homophobia," *Journal of Social Issues* 34, no. 1 (1978): 29–47.

2. These categories were derived from Gregory M. Herek's description of the experiential, defensive, and symbolic functions of homophobia in "Beyond 'Homophobia': A Social Psychological Perspective on Attitudes toward Lesbians and Gay Men," *Journal of Homosexuality* 10, nos. 1/2 (Fall, 1984): 8–13.

3. Ibid., 6–7. Herek's article summarizes a number of studies suggesting that homophobic people report less contact with gays and lesbians; tend to be older, more religious, and less educated; subscribe to rigid sex roles and feel more guilt about sexuality; tend to be more authoritarian; and oppose civil rights for other minorities. Men tend to be more homophobic than women.

4. A study by Rodney Karr, "Homosexual Labeling: An Experimental Analysis," showed that men were perceived as more masculine when they labeled someone homosexual (Ph.D. diss., University of Washington, 1975). Cited in Morin and Garfinkle, "Male Homophobia": 41.

5. The U.S. Supreme Court upheld Georgia's antisodomy statute in Bowers v. Hardwick, 106 S.Ct. 2841 (1986).

6. San Francisco and Seattle have both adopted ordinances that allow same-sex partners to register as domestic partners. For information on protecting your legal rights through wills, sample contracts, and powers of attorney, see Hayden Curry and Denis Clifford, *The Legal Guide for Lesbian and Gay Male Couples* (Berkeley: Nolo Press, 1989).

7. Allan Berube, *Coming Out Under Fire—The History of Gay Men and Women in World War II* (New York: Free Press, 1990), 2.

8. In January 1991, Health and Human Services Secretary Louis Sullivan recommended that AIDS and HIV be removed from the list of communicable diseases used to bar aliens from entry into the United States. As of this writing, however, the ban is still in effect. The exclusion of tourists and immigrants on the basis of sexual orientation was also eliminated.

9. During the hearings for funding the National Endowment for the Arts in 1990, an antiobscenity oath was considered as a requirement (and later dropped) in response to the controversy surrounding the exhibit of photography by Robert Mapplethorpe. Dennis Barrie, director of the Contemporary Arts Center in Cincinnati, was charged with obscenity (and later acquitted) for sponsoring this exhibit.

10. In October 1986, Pope John Paul II sent a letter to the American bishops that referred to a "homosexual inclination" as an "objective moral disorder." See David F. Greenberg, *The Construction of Modern Homosexuality* (Chicago: University of Chicago Press, 1988), 468. The American bishops later clarified their stand, stating that it was not homosexuality per se that was evil (since gay people did not really choose to be gay), but that homosexual *acts* are sinful.

Progressive members within the Catholic, Protestant, and Jewish faiths continue to press for reform, with varied success. See notes for chapter 5.

11. Sarah Diamond, *Spiritual Warfare—The Politics of the Christian Right* (Boston: South End Press, 1989). Diamond documents right-wing religious efforts to oppose civil rights for gay people.

12. See Sylvia Pennington, *Ex-Gays—There Are None!* (Hawthorne, Calif.: Lambda Christian Fellowship, 1989). An exposé of ex-gay ministries.

13. The Hate Crimes Statistics Bill of 1990 in the U.S. Congress added gay-bashing to the list of reportable crimes.

14. Some studies suggest that even people who are extremely homophobic may be influenced by exposure to ideas that counter homophobic assumptions. See J. Serdahely and G. J. Ziemba, "Changing Homophobic Attitudes Through College Sexuality Education," *Journal of Homosexuality* 10, nos. 1/2 (Fall, 1984).

15. See L. Festinger, *A Theory of Cognitive Dissonance* (Evanston, Ill.: Row, Peterson, 1957).

16. This formulation was adapted from the model, Oppression + Lies + Isolation = Alienation, in H. Wyckoff, *Solving Women's Problems* (New York: Grove Press, 1977). I am grateful to Judith Pohl, who cited this model in her paper "Beyond Internalized Oppression: Theory, Manifestations, Healing, and Research" for her doctoral comprehensives (Georgia State Univer-

sity, 1988). She also provided an extensive bibliography on internalized oppression.

17. Paul Gibson documented a suicide attempt rate of 20 percent to 35 percent among lesbian and gay youth. His article, "Gay Male and Lesbian Youth Suicide," was submitted to Secretary of Health and Human Services Margaret Heckler's Commission on Youth Suicide. The report recommended that we legislate against antigay violence and stop condemning homosexuality. Although his article was included in the final report, it was disavowed by secretary Louis Sullivan in response to antigay protests. *Report of the Secretary of Health and Human Services Task Force on Youth Suicide* (Washington, D.C.: Health and Human Services, no. ADM (89-1624), Volume 3, 1989). Gibson's paper is also scheduled to appear in an upcoming volume of the *Journal of Homosexuality*. For citations of other studies documenting the rate of gay youth and suicide, see A. Martin and E. Hetrick, "The Stigmatization of the Gay and Lesbian Adolescent," *Journal of Homosexuality 15,* nos. 1/2 (1988): 172.

18. The march on Washington for gay and lesbian rights in 1987, one of the largest marches for civil rights in U.S. history (400,000 participants), was ignored by the major news media.

19. Evelyn Hooker, "The Adjustment of the Male Overt Homosexual," *Journal of Projective Techniques* 21 (1957): 18–31.

20. A. Bell, M. Weinberg, and S. Hammersmith, *Sexual Preference— Its Development in Men and Women* (Bloomington, Ind.: Indiana University Press, 1981), 76.

21. Ibid. See also Richard Green, *The "Sissy Boy" Syndrome and the Development of Homosexuality* (New Haven: Yale University Press, 1987).

22. Richard A. Isay, *Being Homosexual—Gay Men and Their Development* (New York: Farrar, Straus & Giroux, 1990), 34. For additional insight into current psychoanalytic thinking about homosexuality, see Richard Friedman, *Male Homosexuality—A Contemporary Psychoanalytic Perspective* (New Haven: Yale University Press, 1988).

23. For a discussion of "essentialists" and "social constructionists," see James Weinrich, *Sexual Landscapes—Why We Are What We Are, Why We Love Whom We Love* (New York: Charles Scribner's Sons, 1987), 82–107. He suggests that we can better understand homosexual development by looking at the interaction of both heredity and environment.

24. For a description of the effects of homophobic conditioning on both gay and heterosexual men, see Franklin Abbott, ed., *Men and Intimacy— Personal Accounts Exploring the Dilemmas of Modern Male Sexuality* (Freedom, Calif.: Crossing Press, 1990).

25. "Accepting one's physique and learning to cope with a masculine or feminine role" was the first of nine developmental tasks in Robert J. Havighurst, *Developmental Tasks and Education* (New York: Longmans, Green, 1951), 30–55.

26. I derived this description of stages from a combination of current theories and from my own observations while running a support group for gay adolescents over a period of seven years. For a comparative description of various models of homosexual identity formation, see Richard Troiden, "The Formation of Homosexual Identities," *Journal of Homosexuality* 17, nos. 1/2 (1988): 43–74.

2: Dysfunctional and Abusive Families

1. See J. Patrick Gannon, *Soul Survivors—A New Beginning for Adults Abused as Children* (New York: Prentice Hall, 1989); John Bradshaw, *Bradshaw on: The Family—A Revolutionary Way of Self-Discovery* (Deerfield Park, Fla,: Health Communications, 1988); and Claudia Black, *Double-Duty—Dual Dynamics Within the Chemically Dependent Home* (New York: Ballantine, 1990), which offers help for the child of a substance-abusing family who is also food-addicted, disabled, sexually abused, an only child, chemically dependent, a person of color, physically abused, gay or lesbian, or whose parents are both chemically dependent.

Another resource for survivors with a helpful workbook format is Ellen Rather, *The Other Side of the Family—A Book for Recovery from Abuse, Incest, and Neglect* (Deerfield Park, Fla.: Health Communications, 1990).

2. D.W. Winnicott, *Playing and Reality* (New York: Basic Books, 1971), 111–18. Winnicott describes the "good enough mother" (or caretaker) who is able to "mirror" or reflect her child's true self (in contrast to a parent who feels threatened by her child's feelings). Although she may not always be in tune with her child's every need, she is generally able to empathize with his feelings and experience.

3. Alice Miller, *For Your Own Good—Hidden Cruelty in Child-Rearing and the Roots of Violence* (New York: Farrar, Straus & Giroux, 1983). Miller describes how parents rationalize their abuse by declaring that it's for the child's own good.

4. Parenting guides are available that demonstrate numerous ways to set appropriate limits with children without using physical punishment. See Thomas Gordon, *Parents Effectiveness Training* (New York: Wyden Books, 1977).

3: Effects of Abuse on Gay Sexuality

1. Mic Hunter, *Abused Boys—The Neglected Victims of Sexual Abuse* (Lexington, Mass.: Lexington Books, 1990), 26. Hunter cites studies that document a range of 2.5 percent to 16 percent, although sexual abuse of boys is underreported.

2. Mike Lew, *Victims No Longer—Men Recovering from Incest and Other Sexual Child Abuse* (New York: Harper & Row, 1988), 61.

Both *Victims No Longer* and *Abused Boys* are important resources for men who were sexually abused as children. They include stories written by gay male survivors and a few stories from men who were sexually abused by women. See also *The Sexually Abused Male, Volumes I and II*. Mic Hunter, ed. (Lexington, Mass: Lexington Books, 1990).

A book for women that includes many helpful suggestions that are also applicable to men is Ellen Bass and Laura Davis, *The Courage to Heal: A Guide for Women Survivors of Child Sexual Abuse* (New York: Harper & Row, 1988). See also Laura Davis, *The Courage to Heal Workbook: For Women and Men Survivors of Child Sexual Abuse* (Harper & Row, New York, 1990).

3. European age-of-consent laws stipulate the following minimum ages for male homosexual contact: fourteen in Italy and Albania; fifteen in Denmark, France, Greece, Poland, and Sweden; sixteen in Belgium, Holland, Portugal, Norway, and Switzerland; eighteen in Luxembourg, Germany, Austria, Czechoslovakia, Finland, and Hungary; twenty-one in Britain and Bulgaria; illegal in Ireland, Romania, and the Soviet Union. From Shelley Anderson, "Falling Borders, Rising Hopes: Europe in 1992," *Out/Look, Lesbian and Gay Quarterly*, no. 10 (Fall, 1990): 32. Compiled from *Hosi-Wien* and from the International Lesbian and Gay Association.

4. Exceptions to the incest taboo include cultures where incest takes on a ritualized function, such as royal siblings in ancient Egypt.

5. "Then there was the astonishing thing that in every case . . . blame was laid on perverse acts by the father . . . though it was hardly credible that perverted acts against children were so general." Sigmund Freud, *The Origins of Psychoanalysis: Letters to Wilhelm Fliess, Drafts and Notes: 1887–1902* (Basic Books: New York, 1954), 217.

For a critique of Freud's shift in his assessment of incest stories, see J. Masson, *The Assault on Truth: Freud's Suppression of the Seduction Theory* (New York: Farrar, Straus & Giroux, 1984). See also Alice Miller, *Thou Shalt Not Be Aware—Society's Betrayal of the Child* (New York: New American Library, 1984).

6. Roland Summit, "The Child Sexual Abuse Accommodation Syndrome," *Child Abuse and Neglect* 7:2 (1983): 182.

7. See Richie McMullen, *Male Rape—Breaking the Silence on the Last Taboo* (London: Gay Men's Press, 1990), 118.

8. Ritual abuse may include the use of restraints, being forced to eat one's own waste, skinning animals alive, being buried alive, witnessing and being forced to participate in the rape of children, castration, torture, and murder. See Larry Kahner, *Cults That Kill* (New York: Random House, 1988).

9. Eli Coleman, "The Development of Male Prostitution Activity Among Gay and Bisexual Adolescents," in Gilbert Herdt, ed., *Gay and Lesbian Youth* (New York: Haworth Press, 1989), 140–41. The author cites numerous studies linking male prostitution to early sexual abuse.

See also M. H. Silbert and A. M. Pines, "Child sexual abuse as an antecedent to prostitution," *Child Abuse and Neglect* 5 (1981): 407–11; and D. K. Weisberg, *Children of the Night—A Study of Adolescent Prostitution* (Lexington, Mass.: Lexington Press, 1984).

10. Peter Rutter, *Love in the Forbidden Zone* (Los Angeles: J. P. Tarcher, 1989).

To report sexual abuse by helping professionals, contact the licensing board in your state. They can explain your options for filing criminal charges or a civil suit and tell you where to seek help to deal with the aftereffects of such abuse. You can also report the abuse to the professional association of your abuser. See Valerie Quinn, *Professional Therapy* NEVER *Includes Sex* (Sacramento: Department of Consumer Affairs, 1990). To order a copy of this pamphlet, write to the DCA, 1020 N Street, Sacramento, CA 95814.

11. J. Briere, D. Evans, M. Runtz and T. Wall, "Symptomatology in Men Who Were Molested as Children: A Comparison Study," *American Journal of Orthopsychiatry* 58(3), July 1988.

Mic Hunter identifies factors that may influence the impact of sexual abuse: how coercive, threatening, and violent it was; how early it started, how frequent it was, and how long it lasted; how may adults took part and what their relationships were to the child; and how other adults reacted to the abuse (*Abused Boys*, 45–46).

12. For a comparison of effects identified in research studies of sexual abuse survivors, see the appendix in John Briere, *Therapy for Adults Molested as Children—Beyond Survival* (New York: Springer Publishing Company, 1989).

13. J. James and J. Meyerding, "Early Sexual Experience as a Factor in Prostitution," *Archives of Sexual Behavior* 7 (1978): 31–42. This source was

cited by Coleman (see note 9): "These authors concluded that childhood sexual assault serves as a premature introduction into adult sexuality and teaches the child to use sex to meet adolescent non-sexual needs."

14. R. Summit, "The Child Sexual Abuse Accommodation Syndrome," 177. He cites five elements of the child sexual abuse accommodation syndrome that inhibit a child's ability to disclose the abuse: (1) secrecy, (2) helplessness, (3) entrapment and accommodation, (4) delayed, unconvincing disclosure, and (5) retraction.

15. Wendy Malt and Beverly Holman, *Incest and Sexuality—A Guide to Understanding and Healing* (Lexington, Mass.: Lexington Books, 1987), 17. This book also has a section describing the effect of sexual abuse on the sexuality of male incest survivors.

16. "Correlations linking abuse with adult homosexuality should not be interpreted as a cause-and-effect relationship that results in adult homosexual preference." From Debra Boyer, "Male Prostitution and Homosexual Identity," in Herdt, ed., *Gay and Lesbian Youth*, 180–81.

4: Post-Traumatic Stress

1. See S. Eth and R. S. Pynoos, eds., *Post-Traumatic Stress Disorder in Children* (Washington, D.C.: American Psychiatric Press, 1985); and M. Horowitz, *Stress Response Syndromes* (New York: Jason Aronson, 1976).

2. *Diagnostic and Statistical Manual of Mental Disorders*, 3d edit., rev. (DSM-III-R), Post-traumatic stress disorder (Washington, D.C.: American Psychiatric Association, 1987), 309.89.

3. See Truddi Chase, *When Rabbit Howls* (New York: Jove, 1990). A first-person account of multiple personality; and Frank Putnam, *Diagnosis and Treatment of Multiple Personality Disorder* (New York: Gilford Press, 1989).

4. See Gershen Kaufman, *The Psychology of Shame—Theory and Treatment of Shame-Based Syndromes* (New York: Springer, 1989), 51. Kaufman describes how suppression of feelings can cause endocrine changes, which may result in psychosomatic illness.

5. Rollo May, *The Meaning of Anxiety* (New York: Norton, 1977). May reports on a study of the relation between anxiety and rejection in a group of unmarried mothers: "The proletarian mothers rejected their children, but they never made any bones about it. The children knew they were rejected; they went out on the streets and found other companions. . . . But the middle class young women were always lied to in their families. *They were rejected by*

mothers who pretended they loved them. This was the source of their anxiety, not the sheer rejection.'' [emphasis added]

Cited in ''Creativity and the Unconscious'' in O. Bertagnolli and J. Rackham, eds., *Creativity and the Writing Process* (New York: John Wiley, 1982, 21.

6. Walt Odets, ''The Psychological Epidemic: The Impact of AIDS on Uninfected Gay and Bisexual Men,'' 50. Paper presented at the International AIDS Forum, San Francisco, June 1990.

7. Michael Bridges, ''Appreciating the Trauma: Post-Traumatic Stress and the AIDS Care Provider.'' Paper presented at the eleventh National Lesbian and Gay Health Conference, San Francisco, April 1989.

5: Self-Blame and Shame

1. ''While guilt is a painful feeling of regret and responsibility for one's actions, shame is a painful feeling about oneself as a person.'' Merle Fossum and Marilyn Mason, *Facing Shame—Families in Recovery* (New York: W. W. Norton, 1986), 5.

2. John Bradshaw refers to a ''healthy'' form of shame, which recognizes our human imperfection. I prefer to call this recognition ''humility'' and reserve the word *shame* for describing a core sense of being defective or unworthy. John Bradshaw, *Healing the Shame That Binds You* (Deerfield, Fla: Health Communications, 1988), 3.

3. See John Boswell, *Christianity, Social Tolerance, and Homosexuality* (Chicago: University of Chicago Press, 1980); Chris Glaser, *Come Home! Reclaiming Spirituality and Community as Gay Men and Lesbians* (San Francisco: Harper & Row, 1990); Richard Hasbany, ed., *Homosexuality and Religion* (New York: Haworth Press, 1990); Malcolm Boyd, *Are You Running With Me, Jesus?—A Spiritual Companion for the 1990s* (Boston: Beacon Press, 1990); and Christie Balka and Andy Rose, eds., *Twice Blessed—On Being Lesbian, Gay and Jewish* (Boston: Beacon Press, 1990).

4. See Aldous Huxley, *The Perennial Philosophy* (New York: Harper and Brothers, 1945).

5. Metropolitan Community Church was one of the first Christian churches specifically for gay people. Gays have also formed groups derived from other denominations: Dignity, for Catholics; Integrity, for Episcopalians; Emerge, for Christian Scientists; Affirmation, for Mormons; and Acceptance, for Baptists. Groups also exist for Lutherans, Presbyterians, Jews, Evangelicals, and others.

6. The American Friends Service Committee of the Religious Society of Friends (Quakers) has an affirmative action program for gay people. The United Church of Christ and Unitarians have accepted openly gay people as members of their clergies.

7. For a description of the pagan rituals of the "radical fairies," see Stuart Timmons, *The Trouble with Harry Hay: Founder of the Modern Gay Movement* (Boston: Alyson, 1990). See also Judy Grahn, *Another Mother Tongue—Gay Words, Gay Worlds* (Boston: Beacon Press, 1984).

8. Winnicott used the term "false self" to describe the adaptive response of a child to the unconscious needs of his parents. I have extended this definition to include these other strategies for coping with an abusive family, because they also distort the natural growth of the child. D. W. Winnicott, *Maturational Processes and the Facilitating Environment: Studies in the Theory of Emotional Development* (Madison, Conn.: International Universities Press, 1965), 140–52.

9. For a description of identifying with the aggressor and other defense mechanisms, see Anna Freud, *Ego and the Mechanisms of Defense* (Madison, Conn.: International Universities Press, 1967).

6: Origins of Self-Destructive Behavior

1. Robert J. Kus, "Alcoholism and Non-Acceptance of Gay Self: The Critical Link," *Journal of Homosexuality* 15, nos. 1/2 (1988): 25. Kus cites a number of studies supporting this statistic. His own study suggests that nonacceptance of a positive gay identity may contribute to alcoholism.

2. Jonathan Shedler and Jack Block, "Adolescent Drug Use and Psychological Health: A Longitudinal Inquiry," *American Psychologist* 45 (May 1990): 612–30.

3. Patrick Carnes, *Contrary to Love: Healing the Sexual Addict* (Minneapolis: CompCare, 1989), 127. Carnes describes the assumptions of the sexual addict in the following terms: I'm worthless, no one could ever love me, my needs will never be met by others, sex is my most important need, and I'm bad because sex is my most important need. See also Carne's two other books: *Out of the Shadows: Understanding Sexual Addiction* (Minneapolis: CompCare, 1983) and *Don't Call it Love—Recovery from Sexual Addiction* (New York: Bantam, 1991).

See other listings in note 3, chapter 8.

4. P. Clance, *The Imposter Phenomenon—When Success Makes You Feel Like a Fake* (Atlanta: Peachtree, 1985). See also David Tresemer, *The Fear of Success* (New York: Plenum, 1977).

5. Alice Miller, *Drama of the Gifted Child—the Search for the True Self* (New York: Basic Books, 1981), 43–44. Miller describes the need to mourn for early deficits.

6. *Ibid.*, 39. "One is free from depression when self-esteem is based on authenticity of one's own feelings and not on the possession of certain qualities."

7. The Marin (California) Domestic Violence Project calls this devastated feeling the "fatal peril."

8. Gail Golden and Phyllis Frank, "Blaming by Naming: The Epidemic of Codependency and the Battered Woman." Paper presented at the Twelfth National Lesbian and Gay Health Conference, Washington, D.C., July 1990.

9. *Ibid.* Research on domestic violence suggests that people from many different backgrounds are battered.

10. David Island and Patrick Letellier, *Men Who Beat the Men Who Love Them—Battered Gay Men and Domestic Violence* (Binghamton, New York: Haworth Press, 1991). This book provides valuable resources for gay men who have been battered.

11. Timmen Cermak, *Diagnosing and Treating Co-Dependence* (Minneapolis: Johnson Institute, 1986). Cermak makes a case for including codependence in the Diagnostic and Statistical Manual for Mental Disorders. Other studies show that people can exhibit codependent features without codependency being a permanent part of their personality structure (see Fossum and Mason, *Facing Shame*).

Codependent behavior takes place on a continuum: Some people occasionally defer to others even if it's not in their own best interests, while others may seriously neglect their needs in a desperate attempt to preserve a dysfunctional relationship.

Other codependency resources include Pia Mellody, *Facing Codependency—Where It Comes From, How It Sabotages our Lives* (San Francisco: Harper & Row, 1989); and Melody Beattie, *Codependent No More* (New York: Harper/Hazelden, 1987).

12. D. Sondin and M. Durphy, *Learning to Live Without Violence—A Handbook for Men* (San Francisco: Volcano Press, 1985).

8: Recovery from Addictions and Compulsions

1. According to *Smoking Tobacco and Health: Fact Book* (Atlanta: Center for Disease Control, 1989), tobacco-related deaths in the United States are estimated to be close to 400,000 a year. Alcohol-related deaths are more than 100,000 a year; see *Report to Congress on Alcoholism and Health* (Washington, D.C.: National Institute on Alcohol Abuse and Alcoholism, 1987).

An exact comparison with illegal substance abuse death rates is difficult because the statistics are not compiled in the same way. The following drug-related medical emergencies were reported to the Drug Abuse Warning Network by the emergency rooms of 400 hospitals in 27 metropolitan areas in 1988: cocaine, 3,618; alcohol in combination with other drugs, 2,778; heroin and morphine, 2,746; marijuana, 246; hallucinogens, 213 (Washington D.C., National Institute on Drug Abuse, 1989).

2. For vivid descriptions of "hitting bottom" and recovery, see Robert F. Kus, *Gay Men of Alcoholics Anonymous—First-Hand Accounts* (North Liberty, Iowa: Winterstar Press, 1990).

3. Two other excellent resources for gay men who are following the twelve-step model of recovery are Sheppard Kominars, *Accepting Ourselves—The Twelve-Step Journey of Recovery from Addiction for Gay Men and Lesbians* (San Francisco: Harper & Row, 1989); and David Crawford, *Easing the Ache—Gay Men Recovering from Compulsive Behaviors* (New York: Dutton, 1990).

Other resources for recovery from sexual compulsion: (Anonymous), *Hope and Recovery: A Twelve-Step Guide to Healing from Compulsive Sexual Behavior* (Minneapolis CompCare). Mic Hunter and "Jim," a recovering codependent. *The First Step: For People in Relationships with Sex Addicts* (Minneapolis, CompCare). *Sex and Love Addicts Anonymous* (Boston: Augustine Fellowship, 1986).

See other listings in note 3, chapter 6.

4. James Christopher, *How to Stay Sober—Recovery Without Religion* (Buffalo, N.Y.: Prometheus Books, 1988). For another non–twelve-step guide to recovery, see Stanton Peele and Archie Brodsky, *The Truth About Addiction and Recovery* (New York: Simon & Schuster, 1991).

5. See Earnie Larsen, *Stage II Recovery—Life Beyond Addiction* (San Francisco: Harper & Row, 1985).

6. Robert J. Kus, "Alcoholism and Non-Acceptance of Gay Self: The Critical Link," *Journal of Homosexuality* 15, nos. 1/2 (1988): 39. Kus's study suggests that sobriety can lead to acceptance of your sexual orientation with the support of other gay men in recovery.

7. Kent Jarratt, "The Use of Ericksonian Hypnotherapy in Work with the Sexually Compulsive/Addicted Client." Paper presented at the Twelfth National Lesbian and Gay Health Conference, Washington, D. C., July 1990. Jarratt describes how the relationship with a psychotherapist constructs a nonshaming holding environment, which can counter the self-reinforcing cycle of shame. His paper will be published in the *American Journal of Preventive Psychiatry and Neurology*.

8. Alcoholics Anonymous grew out of the Oxford Group Movement, originally known as the First Century Christian Fellowship and later as Moral Re-Armament. Frank Buchanan, the founder of the Oxford Group Movement, developed the ideas that later became a major part of AA and other twelve-step programs. These include self-examination, acknowledgment of character defects, restitution for harm done to others, recounting one's life story, and accepting divine inspiration. See Jim Orford, *Excessive Appetites: A Psychological View of Addictions* (New York: John Wiley and Sons, 1985), 301–2.

9. St. John of the Cross, *The Dark Night of the Soul* (Garden City, N.Y.: Doubleday, 1959). The author describes the feeling of utter hopelessness and abandonment that came prior to his sense of union with God. Cited in Linda Schierse Leonard, *Witness to the Fire—Creativity and the Veil of Addiction* (Boston: Shambhala, 1989). Leonard's book looks at the crisis of meaning experienced in recovery and compares it with the archetypal experience of the creative process.

The process of recovery can also be likened to a mythic quest: You set out on a voyage through the strange territory of your emotions, not knowing what fearsome beasts or dragons may await you. As you enter the dark wood of unconscious needs and desires, you may be tempted from your quest by sirens who enchant you with deadly potions or by wizards who try to seduce you. When you're close to achieving your goal, your emotions flare up like a mighty dragon that threatens to devour you. Your support group provides the magic talisman that helps you survive the trials of temptation and tame the wild beast of your emotions. At the top of the pinnacle, you discover your own true self, which was waiting to be revealed to you all along. You bring this self-knowledge down from the mountain and share your boon with others.

For a description of the hero's quest, see Joseph Campbell, *The Hero With a Thousand Faces* (Princeton, N.J.: Princeton University Press, 1949), 36.

9: Working Through Feelings

1. George A. Clum, "Psychological Interventions vs. Drugs in Treatment of Panic," *Behavior Therapy* 20 (1989): 429–57.

2. In a study of widows, those who "broke down" in the first week following the death of their husbands showed less physical and psychological symptoms a year later than those who showed no emotion. C. Parkes, *Bereavement* (Madison, Conn.: International Universities Press, 1987).

3. I. Blackburn, S. Bishop, A. Glen, L. Whalley, and J. Christie, "The Efficacy of Cognitive Therapy in Depression. A Treatment Trial Using Cognitive Therapy and Pharmacotherapy, Each Alone and in Combination," *British Journal of Psychiatry* 139 (January 1981): 181–89. This study showed that the combination of antidepressant drugs with cognitive therapy was more effective with severe, refractory depression than either modality used alone.

4. For a more elaborate description of developing awareness as a meditative or spiritual discipline, see Joseph Goldstein and Jack Kornfield, *Seeking the Heart of Wisdom—The Path of Insight Meditation* (Boston: Shambhala, 1987).

10: Self-Nurturing

1. For other examples of distortions in thinking, see Matthew McKay and Patrick Fanning, *Self-Esteem—A Proven Program of Cognitive Techniques for Assessing, Improving, and Maintaining Your Self-Esteem* (Oakland, Calif.: New Harbinger, 1987), 198–200; David Burns, *Feeling Good—The New Mood Therapy* (New York: New American Library, 1980), 40–41; and Albert Ellis and Robert Harper, *A New Guide to Rational Living* (North Hollywood: Wilshire Book Company, 1975), 198–200.

2. *Ibid.*, 119. Ellis and Harper call this sequence the ABC of rational emotive therapy: the Activating event, your Belief system about the event, and the emotional Consequence.

3. For a discussion of panic, despair, and quality of life in response to AIDS, see the section on suicidal thoughts in chapter 10 of Rik Isensee, *Love Between Men* (New York: Prentice Hall Press, 1990), 144–47.

11: Seeking Support

1. For some tips on finding a gay-sensitive therapist, see Marny Hall, *The Lavender Couch* (New York: Alyson, 1985). Also, Robert J. Kus, *Keys to Caring: Assisting Your Gay and Lesbian Clients* (Boston: Alyson, 1990).

2. Group treatment for adult survivors may emphasize different aspects of recovery: codependency issues, alcoholic families, communication skill-building, or self-esteem. Some groups are fairly structured around specific topics, while other groups focus on the process of interaction among the members.

3. Carolyn Cole and Elaine Barney, "Safeguards and the Therapeutic Window—A Group Treatment Strategy for Adult Incest Survivors," *American Journal of Orthopsychiatry* 57(4), October 1987: 601–609.

12: Self-Empowerment

1. Y. Amir, "The Role of Intergroup Interaction in Change of Prejudice and Intergroup Relations," in P. Katz, ed., *Towards the Elimination of Racism* (New York: Pergamon Press, 1975). Cited by G. Herek, "Beyond 'Homophobia': A Social Psychological Perspective on Attitudes toward Lesbians and Gay Men," *Journal of Homosexuality* 10, nos. 1/2 (Fall 1984): 14.

Index

▼

Index

▼

C

D

About the Author

▼

R<small>IK</small> I<small>SENSEE</small> is a licensed clinical social worker who has practiced psychotherapy with gay couples for the past thirteen years. For three years he served as clinical supervisor for the Shanti Project in San Francisco, which provides services for people with AIDS and their loved ones. He is the author of *Love Between Men*, a Lambda Book Report bestseller, and *We're Not Alone*, a novel about gay teenagers. He lives in San Francisco.